Heritage Waterways 2006

Cover picture.
The 'stream in the sky'. Sue Mills.

A Perceptive Images © publication for Mortons Media Group Ltd
May 2006

Written, compiled and edited by Keith Langston

Picture Editor
Sue Mills
Additional editorial material Alan Barnes, Mike Clarke, Justine Lee, Jonathan Ludford, Roger Murray, The specially commissioned aerial pictures were taken using kites by James Gentles.
www.gentles.info/KAP
With thanks to British Waterways, Waterways Ireland, Waterways Trust, Broads Authority, Inland Waterways Association, Association of Canal Cruising Clubs, Association of Inland Navigation Authorities, Inland Waterways Association of Ireland, Scottish Inland Waterways Association

Designers
Charlotte Ball
Anita Tams-Waters
Cover Design
Darren Hendley

Publisher
Dan Savage
Publishing Director
Malcom Wheeler
Finance Director
Brian V Hill
Managing Director
Terry Clark

Published by
Mortons Media Group Ltd, Media Centre, Morton Way, Horncastle Lincolnshire LN9 6JR
Tel. 01507 523456
www.classicmagazines.co.uk

Printed by
William Gibbons & Son, Wolverhampton

MORTONS Media Group Ltd

A valuable inheritance!

Above: An aptly named boat sails into the basin below Chirk Tunnel on the Llangollen Canal. *Tranquillity* is one of the main reasons for the popularity of the waterways. Sue Mills.

In this 21st century, navigable inland waterways are attractive and unique lateral theme parks. They traverse in England, Scotland and Wales some 3000 miles (3218km) and on the island of Ireland a further 621 miles (1000km). The rivers and canals that make up those waterways are individual treasure troves of fascinating rural and urban landscapes just waiting to be explored by boat, on foot or by cycle.

In over 50 years of intense activity, the pioneering canal builders opened up the countryside to travel on a scale never before seen. While doing so they also improved natural watercourses, many of which were then connected into the new and revolutionary transport system. As the great rivers were interconnected one with the other, so the deep water sea ports were also made more accessible to traders from inland areas.

As early as 1556, the Exeter Ship Canal was created and that river improvement, made to allow the easier passage of cargo vessels, is said to have been the first to utilise weirs and locks, albeit with vertically rising gates. However, the real canal building boom was still 200 years away!

Interestingly, the islands of Britain may have seen the building of canals in order to allow navigation by boat long before the so-called industrial era. The Romans are said to have experienced difficulty in making any of the rivers to the west of Lincoln (Lindum Colonia) navigable. They accordingly built Foss Dyke which, if, as some historians claim, it was built to allow those invaders to sail west to the River Trent, would make it by far and away the earliest artificial navigation constructed within these islands.

Furthermore that waterway was said to have been treated to its 'channel being scoured' in 1121 during the reign of Henry I in order to improve navigation. So did those contractors to the King, under the guidance of one Bishop Atwater, simply rebuild the original Roman cut or dig a new one? If the answer is, as seems likely, to be the former, then the work is surely

the earliest reported instance of canal restoration! That is, thankfully, nowhere near the end of that story as the Fossdyke & Witham Navigation can still be sailed to this day.

In 1759 the third Duke of Bridgwater, Francis Edgerton, returned to the north-west of England having made a trip to France, where he had witnessed first-hand the usefulness to traders of the Canal du Midi. As a consequence of that he decided to enter the canal-building business.

That gentleman saw waterway utilisation as the perfect answer to his major logistical problem – transporting coal from his mines in Worsley to his customers in the mills and homes of industrial Manchester. In perfecting a suitable system, he not only halved the price of his coal but made a great deal of money while doing so. Others with entrepreneurial aspirations witnessed his success and looked enviously at his growing wealth.

What followed has been described by many as 'a scramble', undoubtedly one kick-started by the Duke of Bridgwater's success. For the

following 50 or so years, many fortunes were made as navigations were dug. Specific areas particularly benefited from the coming of the canals. For example, the potteries of Staffordshire and the industrial areas of the Black Country expanded and prospered in a manner no one could previously have imagined possible before the coming of the cuts!

Now supporting thousands of leisure boats, the improved and expanded waterways were perhaps more importantly once the arteries through which the lifeblood of the nation flowed. They not only helped to bring sustenance to millions but also provided work for thousands. To service the boat traffic, an infrastructure of canal builders and repairers, boat builders/repairers and chandlers quickly evolved and, by 1780, it was true to say that Britain was on the move, by water!

From the mid-18th century onward, and until the coming of the railways in about 1845, the river navigations and canals of the UK were the bellows that fanned brightly the fires of the

Top: There are many day trip boats available for hire all over the waterways system. This is *Rosie* owned by Anglo Welsh. Sue Mills.

Above: Once Britain's largest inland port, Bugsworth Basin became disused in 1927. Thanks to the efforts of the Inland Waterways Protection Society and financial assistance from local councils and the EEC, the basin was reopened on 3 August 1999. Bugsworth Basin is classed as an ancient monument. Author.

industrial revolution. Canal freight traffic continued and good tonnages were carried well into the 20th century but, for mass transit freight, the die was cast following the building of the railways.

Boat travel in its heyday opened up the country and huge amounts of cargo were carried from the burgeoning factories to consumers in the UK and via the docks, after being transferred to ocean-going vessels, then exported to all corners of the developing world. Cheshire salt, Lancashire cotton, Yorkshire wools, coal and tar products, china clay, timber, iron ore, foodstuffs and, of course, manufactured goods were all transported by the waterways.

The construction of most of Britain's canals was completed by the early 1800s, but who were the individuals at the behest of the businessmen and investors who actually made it all happen? Well, in the very beginning after the surveys had been made and the capital raised, the first of millions of 'sods' had to be cut, and thereafter literally thousands of canal structures built. The hard men employed to undertake that work were named navvies, a title taken from the word navigator.

Many of the navvies came from Scotland and Ireland but there were also navvies from England and Wales and often they fought fiercely, mainly over national differences and especially when fired up by strong drink!

It was a rough life and the men, sometimes with their family in tow, moved from 'digging' to 'digging', living in conditions which, if they were improved tenfold, would still not be tolerated today. They were reputedly given a ration of two

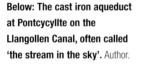

Below: The cast iron aqueduct at Pontcycyllte on the Llangollen Canal, often called 'the stream in the sky'. Author.

pounds of meat, two pounds of bread and five quarts of ale a day and, by the standards of the time, they were quite well paid. At the end of the canal-building era gangs of navvies were still able to find employment with the railway builders as, in many ways, the work was similar.

The dress of the navvy was distinctive and they usually wore moleskin trousers, canvas shirts and velveteen square-tailed topcoats. Worthy of mention in this modern age is the fact that there were in those times no power tools, no mechanical diggers and certainly no health and safety regulations! Just blood, sweat, tears and, of course, picks, shovels and blasting powder (later dynamite).

So who were those early canal pioneers? Well, they certainly were not civil engineers, as that title did not exist at the beginning of their labours! That title's origin is, however, attributed to one of their number, who is universally accepted as being the first man to call himself a civil engineer. These are the brief biographies of some engineers who are considered by many to have exerted the most influence during the period known as the 'canal boom'.

One of the best-known is James Brindley (1716-1772) and his name is synonymous with the building of the Bridgwater Canal. He was a millwright by trade who came from humble stock and was born in Chapel-en-le-Frith, Derbyshire. He went on to work as senior engineer on the Trent & Mersey Canal, and among the many waterways linked with his name are the Droitwich Canal, Staffordshire & Worcestershire Canal, Grand Trunk, Birmingham Canal and the

Chesterfield Canal. Brindley died a comparatively young man at the age of 42; he was reportedly the victim of acute diabetes and overwork.

The Englishman to first use the title civil engineer was John Smeaton (1724-1792). He was born near Leeds and was the son of a solicitor. He started his working life as an instrument maker but, at an early point in that career, became interested in watermills, windmills and other sources of power.

At 29 he became a Fellow of the Royal Society and was responsible for reconstructing the famous Eddystone lighthouse. After adding surveying to his attributes, he became involved in canal construction, notably being involved with the Forth & Clyde Canal in Scotland and the Grand Canal in Ireland (with Jessup). He set up the Society of Civil Engineers in 1771.

William Jessup (1745-1814) was the son of a naval engineer and was born in Devonport, near the naval dockyard. Having worked with Jessup's father on the Eddystone lighthouse, Smeaton took the young man under his tutelage following the death of Mr Jessup Snr. He went on to work on both canal building and river navigation schemes in eastern England and the Midlands.

He was associated with the Grand Junction Canal (Grand Union), Ellesmere Canal (Lllangollen) and the Rochdale Canal. Away from waterways, he founded the Butterley Iron Works in 1790 and famously manufactured at that site fish-bellied cast iron rails, a process that marked an important advance in railway development. In modern times the company he founded was responsible for building that modern canal marvel the Falkirk Wheel. Now there is a real waterways pedigree if ever there was one!

Perhaps the best-known of our early engineers is Thomas Telford (1757-1834), who was born in Westerkirk, Scotland. In his early working life he was apprenticed to a stonemason. When time-served he produced work of outstanding quality and those in authority were quick to note his potential.

His work on Somerset House in London and thereafter on Shrewsbury Castle led to his appointment as Surveyor of Public Works for Shropshire. He later became engineer on the Ellesmere Canal under William Jessup and the greatest canal monuments to his genius are the magnificent cast iron aqueducts at Pontcycyllte and Chirk. He was chief engineer on the

Top left: A delightful view of the Peak Forest Canal at Marple. Author.

Top right: Part of the Hatton flight of 21 locks, looking downstream from Canal Lane towards Warwick Cathedral. Grand Union Canal. Author.

Above left: Part of the popular revitalised Bristol Docks area. Author.

Above right: All things to all people, the old docks railway system being used as a stunt practice area by this talented young cyclist. He had first checked to see that no trains were due! Author.

Above: The fantastic
Pontcysyllte Aqueduct, 127ft
above the River Dee in north
Wales. Author.

Liverpool and Birmingham Canal (Shropshire Union) and built the famous Menai suspension bridge between Anglesey and the mainland.

John Rennie (1761-1821) was born in 1761 in Phantassie, East Lothian, Scotland. Being educated at Edinburgh University, he was one of the first of a new type engineer for those times, in that he was university trained. Having worked as a millwright, he became a surveyor and then engineer on the Kennet & Avon Canal. Academic qualifications aside, he apparently overlooked the basic rule of canal building: the highest level of a canal must have sufficient supplies of water with which to continually refresh its levels, after operating locks etc.

For example, Rennie failed to design this into the Kennet & Avon and so steam pumps had to be installed to replace the water used. However, his design of bridges and aqueducts were thought by many to be architecturally impressive and are still often referred to as 'classic'. He also worked as engineer on both the Rochdale and Lancaster Canals.

All the great canal builders were without doubt men of vision – none more so than James Brindley. It is said that, while Brindley was in the middle of the great Bridgwater Canal contract, he had a canal 'vision' of much greater proportions. He envisaged the idea of a great waterway network connecting England's four main navigable rivers – the Mersey, Trent, Severn and Thames. He gave this plan the innovative name The Grand Cross.

It was not until 1789 that Brindley's Grand Cross was completed, 17 years after his death, which occurred while he was surveying the Caldon Canal in Staffordshire in 1772. Brindley caught a chill that went untreated and led to his premature death at the age of 56.

He and the other pioneers inspired a new generation of canal builders, and some who had been Brindley's assistants went on to complete great navigation works of their own. They included Hugh Henshall, who finished the Trent & Mersey Canal after Brindley's demise; the builder of the Oxford Canal, Samuel Simcock; the Welsh canal builder Thomas Dadford; and Robert Whitford, whose successful projects included the Thames & Severn Canal and the Forth & Clyde Canal.

The Grand Cross was finally completed when the Oxford Canal was 'cut' to join the River Thames. The period which followed has been described as 'Canal Mania', with investors anxious to sink money into the building of new canals. Not all were successful, and many investors poured good money after bad in vain attempts to make their fortunes – many schemes going broke long before completion. The year 1793 can perhaps rightly be cited as being the peak of the canal building rush, as in that year Parliament passed at least 25 Acts to build canals.

So within the relatively short space of 50 years, most of Britain's canal system was completed and the records for 1845 show that an incredible 4400 miles of navigation had been cut. More than 2700 locks had been built on them, together with countless thousands of bridges, many tunnels and no small number of aqueducts constructed. More than 3000 miles

of those new waterways were interconnected!

The canals altered the face of Britain and were unquestionably the bedrock on which the Industrial Revolution was founded. However, by 1844 investors were finding new recipients for their affections as the nation was about to be plunged once again into a building mania – the railways were coming. Their successful development would take away from the canal companies their lifeblood. Goods trains would prove to be a lot quicker than narrow boats and barges! The blow dealt to the canal carriers by the railways can be compared to that delivered by the road transport industry to the railways during the 1960s and 70s.

It is interesting to note that a little over 50 per cent of those waterways survive intact, and in fact the vast majority are still navigable. The canal builders' bequest to our nation has now taken the form of linear leisure parks, and their use is growing and diversifying. The towpaths once pummelled by the feet of heavy workhorses are now ideal routes for those who wish to take their pleasure by Shanks' pony and

they are, in the main, found to be easy and relatively safe walking routes.

There are said to be a little over 3.5-million anglers living on the islands of Britain and between them they spend a reputed £350-million-a-year on their pursuit, a great deal of which includes the purchase of bank fees and rod licences (2004). Anglers are perhaps, in terms of sheer all-year-round numbers, the most conspicuous of our waterways users.

There are 30 listed mainland British inland waterways navigation authorities and they manage water routes that are, in the main, all suitable for cruising. Thousands of people spend their annual holidays afloat and an even larger number sample the joys during shorter breaks. A large number of people (since canals ceased to be used for trade) choose to live on the water and, while there are now marked changes in that number's demographic make-up, the total of people making that lifestyle choice is said to be still growing.

In 1948 the canals of the UK were nationalised as, along with the railways and road freight

Top left: Restored historic boats are very much a part of the revitalised waterways. Pictured is *Shackleton No2 Icebreaker* from the Worcester & Birmingham Canal. Author.

Top right: Half the fun of a cruising holiday for the youngsters is in operating the locks. Bunbury staircase lock on the Shropshire Union Canal. Author.

Below: Lins Mill Aqueduct on the Union Canal near Ratho, Edinburgh. James Gentles.

Top left: The glorious Lough Derg on the Shannon Navigation. Author.

Top right: Etruria Industrial Museum in Staffordshire is situated at the junction of the Caldon and Trent & Mersey canals. Author.

Above left: The coming of the railways marked the end for the waterways where commercial traffic was concerned. A steam locomotive on the tourist Churnet Valley Railway crosses the Caldon Canal at Consall Forge. David Gibson.

Above right: Under the Transport Act of 1962 the Government dissolved the then British Transport Commission, and created five new boards, one of which was the British Waterways Board. Author.

services, and they were taken into ownership by a newly created body the British Transport Commission. The commission was formed as part of the Labour Government's nationalisation plans, first proposed in the 1947 Transport Act. In Northern Ireland control of those concerns was given over to the Ulster Transport Authority.

In 1951 the then Conservative Government denationalised most of Britain's road services. Some years later, under the Transport Act of 1962, the Conservative Government dissolved the British Transport Commission and created five new boards – British Railways Board, British Transport Docks Board, British Waterways Board, London Transport Board and the Transport Holding Company.

A multi-million-pound industry has developed to service the needs of those enjoying the pleasures of the many interesting and diverse waterways. Most of those canal and river routes in England, Scotland and Wales are managed and maintained by British Waterways, a public corporation that actively supports their use for leisure and tourism.

The history and background of the natural and man-made assets that are Ireland's waterways are colourful and chequered. While the rivers and lakes of Ireland were formed during the last ice age, work on the first canal, the Newry Canal, commenced in 1731. New networks of canal, lake and river route were established over the following 130 years linking the island from east to west, north to south.

The networks were developed principally for commercial reasons; however, with the advent of the rail networks and later improved road infrastructure, the waterways went into steady decline as commercial enterprises. By the 1950s, commercial traffic on the waterways was all but finished.

In the 1980s, the Canals Act in the South moved responsibility for the canals to the Office of Public Works (OPW). Steps were then taken to administer the waterways not just as navigations but as recreational facilities. The OPW adopted the same policy with regard to the other waterways under its remit: the Shannon and Barrow Navigations.

In the North, the Department of Agriculture in Northern Ireland had responsibility for the waterways. In 1990 that department, in conjunction with the OPW in the South, initiated the restoration of the Shannon-Erne Waterway, a highly successful project completed in 1993.

In 1996, responsibility for the waterways in the South transferred to the Department of Arts, Culture and the Gaeltacht, later the Department of Arts, Heritage, Gaeltacht and the Islands. Finally, in 1999, responsibility for the waterways North and South was transferred to Waterways Ireland.

Of the river and canal systems controlled by WI, the Barrow Navigation has been in use since the early 1700s and the Erne System (in the North) once carried a great deal of freight. The Grand Canal was built between 1756 and 1803 in order to connect Dublin with the mighty River Shannon, and the Royal Canal was developed as an alternative route from Dublin to the Shannon in the early 19th century. The Shannon-Erne Waterway reopened in 1994 after a three-year project returned it to use.

Investment and conservation: suitable bedfellows?

Mike Clarke of Milepost Research has carried out comprehensive Europe-wide studies into industrial heritage in the course of which he has written a concise history of English Canals. Reproduced here is the section on restoration and investment.

European Union money has been vital to the success of many projects. One, in particular, which used European Regional Development Funding, is the Leeds and Liverpool Canal Corridor project to regenerate the economy of an 80-mile corridor of land on either side of the canal in Lancashire and Wigan. The area around the canal contains many old industrial buildings and the decline in traditional industries had led to some dereliction.

The idea of using the canal as a linking theme for regeneration was first promoted by British Waterways in the early 1980s. Together with the local authorities and private investors, they have been able to attract over £200-million for development projects since then, finance coming from both the public and private sectors. Not only have new buildings been erected, but several historic canalside buildings have been restored and converted for new uses.

For example, in Wigan, an industrial museum has been established in old canal warehouses, reflecting the important position

Below: The restored section of Birmingham Main Line is now a busy tourist attraction, looking towards Broad Street. Author.

Top: It is interesting to note that a little over 50 percent of all the waterways built in the UK survived intact, and in fact the vast majority are still in use. Author

Above left: A cheery wave from the 'holiday' skipper of this Shannon hire navigation cruiser. Author.

Above right: Swan Island on the Shannon Erne Waterway. Waterways Ireland.

of the tourism industry in generating new business. In Blackburn a similar warehouse has been converted to a Business Development Centre, offering advice and facilities for small firms, with a former flour mill nearby now used as offices and a television studio, while in Burnley a former textile mill is currently being converted into a hotel. These are just a few examples of old buildings along the canal corridor that have been altered for new leisure and commercial purposes.

Another example of the reuse of industrial monuments is the conversion of the warehouses around Sheffield canal basin. Close to the city centre, they had fallen into disuse and were virtually derelict, but the site was seen as important to the revitalisation of the former steel-making area in the River Don valley. It was hoped to start work in the mid-1980s, but a deterioration in the property market resulted in the withdrawal of the private developer.

In 1988 the Government set up the Sheffield Development Corporation, giving it extensive powers and finances to regenerate the former steel-making district. British Waterways leased the canal basin site to the Development Corporation, and agreed to restore the warehouses and to clean and landscape the basin. Private developers are erecting modern buildings on part of the site, and they will complement the facilities provided by the older buildings.

Restoration work by British Waterways on the warehouse cost £2.4-million, £1.5-million of this coming from the Development Corporation, together with a further £1-million towards work on the basin. They also provided new access roads and car parking. The complex reopened in 1995 and has provided improved public access to the canal and a boatyard, besides office space in prestigious buildings close to the city centre.

Although most of our English canals are now safe from closure, few are used for transporting goods. Over the last 20 years, all canal developments have used the long-established historical and traditional aspects of canals as part of their marketing strategy. As a result, most people in England now perceive canals as small and antiquated, despite the fact that around four-million tons are carried annually on the larger commercial waterways.

Wide publicity for the history of English canals has had a detrimental effect upon attitudes to investment in modern commercial carrying by inland waterways. The small size of England is

also a disadvantage, short journeys being more suited to road transport. Also, as an island race, we have not seen ourselves as an integrated part of Europe. However, as our dependency upon trade with Europe develops and pressure for environmentally sustainable transport increases, it is to be hoped that there will be more interest in improving navigation, particularly on our rivers, to European standards.

Why has the restoration of English canals been so successful? One of the most important reasons must be the pressure exerted by enthusiasts and the IWA over the last 50 years. Firstly, they changed the public's view of canals from that of a derelict eyesore to one where the historical, environmental and leisure benefits were appreciated. Secondly, by positive publicity in the media, they forced national and local government to re-evaluate the position of canals in their planning policies.

This, in turn, allowed finance to become available from public sources for conservation and restoration. The large-scale private investment which followed would certainly not have been forthcoming had not the public authorities already started to conserve and develop canals.

Much has been achieved by English canal restoration in the conservation of industrial monuments and the creation of new businesses, though the process has taken many years and there are still many problems to overcome. Society has developed rapidly over the last 25 years, and it is now less easy to

define precisely the objectives for conservation and restoration. When restoration was first suggested, canals were mainly used by enthusiasts with simple needs. Today they are visited by more and more people who demand easy access and good facilities.

This is expensive, and the cost of using canal facilities has risen dramatically in order to provide a return on this financial investment. It has led to some criticism, particularly from older enthusiasts who have seen the cost of their hobby or business increase at a faster rate than inflation.

They see new business-oriented developments, with their high cost and extensive alterations to old structures, as destroying the very fabric of the canal environment for which they had worked over the years. Increased access to canals has, to some extent, threatened their peace and tranquillity, one of their prime assets in the modern world.

However, is it possible to justify the cost of maintaining old canal structures without increasing usage and income? Would canals have survived without this increase in funding? In a market-led economy, this is the problem for any conservation project.

The very success of canal restoration has, inevitably, led to increased commercial development. The difficulty for planners and historians is to maintain a balance between preserving the integrity of the past and creating a sustainable future. **W**

Above left: British Waterways are responsible for the maintenance of the historic canal structures under their care. The historic 'floating' swing bridge on the River Weaver is seen receiving attention. Author.

Above right: In the 19th century it was possible to travel by boat from London to Littlehampton via Weybridge, Guildford, Pulborough and Arundel. The route was via the rivers Wey and Arun, linked between Shalford in Surrey, and Pallingham in Sussex, by the 23-mile Wey and Arun Canal. There is an active project under way to restore that historic link. Alan Barnes.

The
Waterways
Trust

Bringing history to life

www.thewaterwaystrust.org.uk

The Waterways Trust is a national charity that works with others to promote greater public enjoyment of our inland waterways. By raising funds for waterways restoration and regeneration activities, and operating the three waterways museums, the trust conserves and interprets the environment and heritage of our waterways.

Education, skills and learning

As custodian of the inland waterways collection and archive, the trust operates the three waterways museums at Gloucester, Ellesmere Port and Stoke Bruerne. These museums tell the continuing story of the profound influence of the waterways on social, technological, economic and environmental development in the UK over three centuries.

The inland waterways collection and archive is a national resource for education and research and the trust works with a range of bodies to develop the museums as centres for interpretation, conservation, research and recreation.

Arts, community and access

Improving our waterways so that they are cared for and enjoyed by people from all walks of life is a key aim of The Waterways Trust.

Above: The Waterways Trust is the custodian of a historic collection of inland waterways craft, which are displayed both in and out of the water at three museum sites: Gloucester Docks, Ellesmere Port Boat Museum and Stoke Bruerne. Author.

Top left: Bugsworth Basin in Derbyshire is an outstanding example of canal restoration. Sue Mills.

Top right: Paul Atterbury, an expert on matters Victorian, is seen here during a visit to Gloucester Docks (Paul appears regularly on the BBC's *Antiques Roadshow*). He is a great supporter of the trust, as are many other celebrities, including the actors David Suchet and Timothy West. Author.

Above: The historic Gloucester Docks are among several locations within the UK where inland waterways craft can rub shoulders with their sea-going counterparts. Author.

The charity raises funds and delivers projects that interpret the waterways through the arts, providing opportunities for recreation and enjoyment along our towpaths. Local communities are encouraged to take part in these improvement projects and the trust provides support for people looking to become actively involved in their local waterway.

Environment and conservation

Our inland waterways provide a haven for wildlife. The trust believes in bringing the waterways alive for people and wildlife. Developing, funding and delivering waterway conservation projects, helping improve habitats and the biodiversity of our waterways, and conserving the associated historic structures is of fundamental importance to the trust.

Recreation, health and activity

Walking, cycling, canoeing and boating – our waterways offer a wealth of opportunities for recreation and tourism. By raising funds to enable more people to take part in activities such as these, the trust encourages the use of the waterways to provide healthy activity and leisure for a wide range of people. The charity also works with other organisations to encourage tourism, attracting more people to the waterways.

From working with small, community-based organisations improving their waterways and towpaths to working with partners on large-scale restoration projects, the Waterways Trust takes inspiration from the energy and enterprise that created the waterways and sustains their modern renaissance.

Preserving the past and looking after the present!

P ivotal in the industrial revolution of Britain, moving the country from an agrarian society to the world's first industrialised nation, our inland waterways exerted a profound influence over life for more than 300 years.

Today, the history of our waterways and their crucial importance to the transformation of the country is largely forgotten.

The Waterways Trust, as the guardian of the nationally important inland waterways collection, works to bring the history of our waterways to life through its three museums – The National Waterways Museum at Gloucester, The Canal Museum at Stoke Bruerne and The Boat Museum at Ellesmere Port.

Through interactive displays and exploring working and static boats, the waterways museums at Gloucester, Ellesmere Port and Stoke Bruerne provide an unrivalled opportunity for visitors of all ages to delve into our industrial heritage.

At each site they can discover how boats were made, how canals were created and how complete families managed to work and live aboard barges and narrow boats.

The collection is a unique national asset and has been designated as being of national importance. It dates from the beginning of canal building in the second half of the 18th century to the present day, providing a vital resource helping reconnect people with their past.

Each museum is also located at a site of historical interest. The award-winning National Waterways Museum at Gloucester is housed in a Victorian warehouse at the historic Gloucester Docks. Through an interactive stocks and shares game, visitors explore the journey of the canal industry through time to find out whether their shares will leave them stinking rich or stony broke. Videos narrated by former canal workers are also used to give an insight into the industry.

Housed in a restored corn mill in a picturesque village, The Canal Museum at Stoke Bruerne, near Northampton, vividly portrays the heritage of 300 years of inland waterways. The museum is situated alongside the Grand Union Canal and visitors can watch holiday boats navigating the flight of locks and the historic Blisworth Tunnel.

The Boat Museum at Ellesmere Port is sited on a 200-year-old dock complex on the bank of the River Mersey, close to the Port of Liverpool. This museum houses the largest collection of historic inland waterway craft in Britain, including narrow boats, canal and river barges, icebreakers, tugs and a coaster.

With the collection of canal boats, a working lock and canal workers' cottages, the museum provides a glimpse of what life was like during the heyday of our waterways.

The open-air museum brings to life the many elements that were essential to a successful canal port in the 19th century. In the Pump House, visitors will find the steam-driven pumping engines that supplied the power for the hydraulic cranes and capstans around the dock, and the Power Hall houses a range of engines that supplied the power for a variety of boats and other canal-related activities.

When Ellesmere Port was a working canal port, the blacksmith's forge was where the canal company's ironwork was made. Today the

Above: The historic Gloucester Docks. Author.

Top left: Many of Britain's towns and cities share in the waterways inheritance. This sandstone cutting is right in the centre of Roman heritage-rich Chester, on the Shropshire Union Canal. Sue Mills.

Top right: More and more families are taking to the inland waterways of these islands as one of their holiday options. This is a family holiday scene on the fascinating Macclesfield Canal. Author.

Above right: Scotland's Crinan Canal is a relic of a bygone age and, as such, it is an enjoyable and beautiful relic, set in truly wonderful scenery. Alan McEwen.

forge is used by the museum's resident blacksmith, and examples of his work can be purchased by visitors.

Following a £2-million refurbishment programme, the story of our inland waterways at The Boat Museum has expanded to include a gallery dedicated to exploring the construction of boats housed in the historic Island Warehouse, built in 1871.

How To Build A Boat charts how boats were made from the Iron Age through the 1800s to the present day.

On the upper floor of the Island Warehouse, visitors can find out more about those who lived and worked on the canals through the interactive displays and recorded stories told by surviving members of old canal families.

Canal crafts, including fender making, leather working, painting and rope making, are demonstrated in a specially designated area. And a new exhibition space in the Toll House enables the museum to house temporary and touring exhibitions.

In addition to telling the story of the waterways in imaginative and dynamic ways, each museum strives to keep traditional waterways crafts and skills alive. Courses such as narrow boat decoration, tug and boat handling skills, blacksmithing and rope work are frequently held at each site.

The trust's work is not just about preserving the past. Through events and information at each of the museums, visitors can discover how our waterways are used today for leisure and recreation, and how they provide habitats for a wide range of wildlife.

From interactive displays and family activities to boat trips, there really is something for everyone at the waterways museums. **W**

Donations to help support the charity or its projects can be made online or by calling 0845 0700 710. The Waterways Trust is a registered charity, No 3728156.

The Waterways Trust

Each museum is open daily (except Christmas Day) 10am-5pm and further information can be found at www.thewaterwaystrust.org.uk or by contacting the museums direct:
The National Waterways Museum
The Docks, Gloucester
Tel: 01452 318200

The Boat Museum
South Pier Road, Ellesmere Port, Cheshire
Tel: 0151 3734373

The Canal Museum
Stoke Bruerne, Northants
Tel: 01604 862229

BARTON TURNS MARINA

Barton Turns Marina is situated in the heart of the Inland Waterway network on the Trent & Mersey canal between Burton on Trent and Lichfield close to the Staffordshire village of Barton under Needwood.

It is a privately owned, purpose built marina which stands on a 65 acre site and includes two lakes, new forest plantations, pleasant parkland style walks with a wide range of wildlife to watch and enjoy.

THE MARINA

We have over 230 berths available for permanent and temporary moorings and as a privately owned marina we can offer our customers competitive rates. Our Marina has a happy, caring atmosphere in order to make you and your family feel right at home when visiting or mooring with us. Our friendly team are always here to help.

Facilities

At Barton Turns Marina you will find a full range of services to meet your needs. Our facilities include:
• Secure Long Term Car Park • Security Gates with Pin Code Access • Electricity to each berth and water to all jetties • Full Disabled & Baby Facilities • Hot and Cold Showers • Well stocked Chandlery and Shop • Elsan/Refuse/Waste Oil Disposal • Diesel/Gas/Coal • Pump Out • Laundry with Washer/Dryer • Brokerage • Marine Insurance • Full Docking-Repair and Boat Yard Services

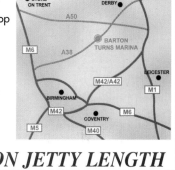

If we can be of any further help to you, please do not hesitate to contact us.

Barton Under Needwood, Burton upon Trent, Staffordshire
DE13 8DZ
Tel: 01283 711666 Fax: 01283 711555
www.bartonturnsmarina.co.uk

MOORING RATE ALL INC. BASED ON JETTY LENGTH

Nottingham

Boat Sales

Leading the way forward

Welcome to Nottingham Boat Sales Limited, one of the UK's leading providers of quality new and pre-owned craft on the inland waterways.

Conveniently located in the city centre of Nottingham we are one of the largest Inland waterways marina's. With years of experience and the unique understanding of the inland waterways network, our aim is to provide a professional service to customers wishing to buy or sell their boat, whether you are a first time buyer, wishing to upgrade your boat or looking to use it for residential purposes - we are the people to see.

We specialise in offering the complete sales package from insurance, finance, organising surveys and moorings. We have an extensive network and relationship with the leading marine finance companies and as a result are able to offer comprehensive and competitive finance packages on all craft.

Call 0115 947 2696 today for free expert advice on all your waterways needs

Nottingham Boat Sales Ltd, Nottingham Castle Marina, Marina Road, Nottingham, NG7 1TN
TEL: 0115 947 2696   FAX: 0115 985 9304   EMAIL: info@notts-boats.co.uk   WEB: www.notts-boats.co.uk

19

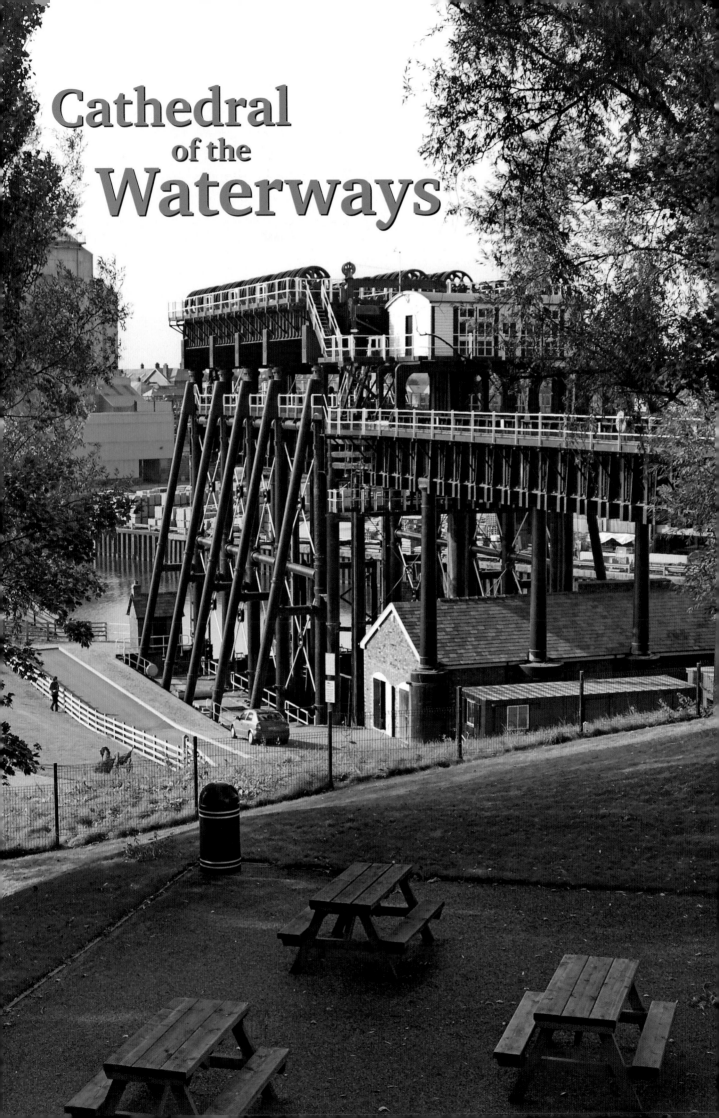

Cathedral
of the
Waterways

Anderton
Boat Lift

The Anderton Boat Lift has been described as both the Cathedral of the Waterways and the Industrial Revolution's greatest waterway wonder. This grand edifice created by Victorian engineering skills underwent a £7-million renovation and was reopened to boat traffic in March 2002 – a simple statement that in itself goes nowhere near to acknowledging the huge community effort that led to its rebuilding.

Future generations may well question whether the grant money, made increasingly available after the inception and proliferation of the Heritage Lottery Fund, was wisely invested on their behalf. In the case of the Anderton Boat Lift, £3.3-million of HLF funding was made available, but perhaps an equally important fact is that more than 2000 private individuals contributed to the scheme,

raising between them a further £430,000.

The success of the appeal, and the resultant rebuilding of the lift, is testament to the affection the local population have for their distinctive Victorian structure. After all, it has been part of the Cheshire scene since 1875 and its uniqueness is something of which Northwich people still proudly boast. But it could so easily have continued to decay, or worse, been allowed to fall into such a state of disrepair that demolition would have become the only option.

Having become unable to be safely operated, the Anderton Lift closed to traffic in 1983.

Such was the intensity of the promotional activities staged by the various groups involved that there was hardly a resident of the Mid-Cheshire area not made aware of the aims and aspirations of those connected with the

Above: The late Fred Dibnah MBE is seen entering the eastern caisson on a narrow boat by way of the aqueduct.
Author.

Anderton Boat Lift Appeal. Perhaps in these times, which we are told herald the beginning of a shrinking lottery pot upon which are to be made even greater and more varying demands, the addition of community self-help of this kind may be the only way to get the job done.

This project was made possible, in part, by the strong partnership forged between the Waterways Trust, the Inland Waterways Association, the Anderton Boat Lift Trust, the Friends of Anderton Boat Lift, the Association of Waterways Cruising Clubs, British Waterways and the Trent and Mersey Canal Society. The fact that the local populace were supportive and enthusiastic must have encouraged the partnership in their endeavours.

The newly restored lift is well used and the modern visitor centre associated with it not only pays its own way but makes a profit. The fee for boat traffic using the facility is included in the cost of the annual waterways boat owners' licence. The subsequent increase in pleasure boat traffic on the Weaver Navigation, having used the lift to travel between the river and the Trent & Mersey Canal, would appear to more than justify this particular investment in our industrial heritage.

The salt industry in Mid-Cheshire was directly responsible for the commercial success of the lift, but ironically that same mineral was, in part, responsible for problems encountered with the structure some 25 years after its introduction. In fact, the 2002 reopening of the lift is a real compliment to the Victorian engineers who originally connected the canal and the river by using a hydraulically powered lift.

The Weaver Navigation engineers at the turn of the century were forced to convert the lift to electrical power following severe corrosion problems. Reverting to the original Victorian concept, the engineers of 2002, albeit with the benefit of modern technology, again rebuilt the lift and configured it to work, once again, hydraulically.

The Anderton Boat Lift exists primarily because of the River Weaver Navigation (a navigation being a river that has been engineered so as to make it navigable). In this case the main driving force behind the lift-building venture was that all-important commodity, salt. Goods were transferred by hand and, in the case of grain and other such suitable materials, by chutes built between the canal and the navigation, a slow and labour intensive process. The need for a more efficient method of transfer became obvious and, described as 'a marvel of its time', the first hydraulically powered boat lift was constructed and opened to traffic in July 1875.

Three Victorian gentlemen are credited with conceiving the idea for a boat lift between the two waterways at Anderton. All notable engineers of the time, they were Edward Leader Williams, John Watt Sandeman and Edwin Clark. The three are said to have collectively persuaded the trustees of the Weaver Navigation to accept the idea of constructing a hydraulic lift. Credit for the final design of the original lift is generally given to Edwin Clark and, when completed, it achieved the engineer's stated aim of transporting boats efficiently between the two waterways without the need for loading and unloading.

The Stockport engineering firm of Emmerson Murgatroyd & Co Ltd was awarded the contract for the fabrication and erection of a lift to carry vessels of canal boat size between the two waterways. The canal was vertically 54ft 4in

Above left: Boats in the eastern caisson. Author.

Above right: Having been lowered, the boats are now at river level and waiting to be allowed to sail out of the lift. Author.

above the level of the river and the initial price for the building of a lift was quoted as being just under £30,000.

The boat lift has two separate 'caissons' (tanks) arranged side-by-side and it is in these that the vessels are carried, together with a suitable amount of water with which to keep them afloat during the transfer. The tanks are referred to respectively as either the western or eastern caisson. Using the principle of hydraulics, the caissons are each supported by a giant ram. Normally the two rams are connected hydraulically, ie with one tank balancing the other. One tank will be raised to the top of the lift (canal level) while the other will be at the bottom of the lift (river level).

Below the aqueduct, which connects the canal with the lift proper and so allows access to the caissons, there is a building that houses the hydraulic equipment. When required, large pumps force the hydraulic fluid from one cylinder (ram) to the other, thereby raising one tank (caisson) while at the same time lowering the other.

On reaching the desired level (river or canal), watertight bulkheads (gates) are raised, allowing the vessel to sail 'free' under its own power and thus gain access to the 'other' waterway. In times of emergency, or during maintenance, one side of the lift could be used in isolation, by using an even bigger pump.

The first lift (1875) used river water to generate such power while the modern version (2002) uses hydraulic oil.

From the old records, it is evident that construction did not run entirely smoothly and an overrun cost in the region of £20,000 was recorded, with the final price of the work invoiced by the contractor being £48,428. Nevertheless, the structure was hailed as being an engineering wonder of the world and pronounced a great success.

By the turn of the century, however, the highly polluted river water, containing as it did a high salt content, was beginning seriously to corrode the machinery and thereby noticeably affect the ability of the lift to operate efficiently.

Accordingly a decision was made to convert

Top left: The aqueduct connecting with the eastern caisson can clearly be seen in this picture. Author.

Top right: The narrow boats now sail free. Author.

Below left: The canal basin at the top of the lift (Trent & Mersey Canal). Author.

Below right: The builder's plate. Author.

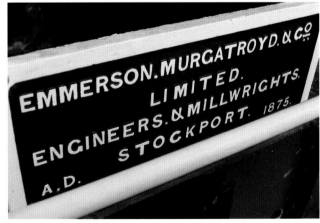

the lift to run on electric power, and this work was undertaken in 1908 under the supervision of Col JA Saner, Engineer to the Weaver Navigation Trustees. The work, which cost £25,869, involved the addition of new headgear and its supporting steelwork, which was built over the existing structure. The installation of electrical control equipment was also required but, such was the intensity of boat traffic constantly waiting to use the lift, only partial closure was allowed during this complex conversion work.

To ensure this, one caisson was converted and then put back into use, after which the other was then similarly treated. At the same time, wire lifting ropes and cast iron counterweights were fitted and new, stronger foundations constructed. This work was demanding and challenging and the colonel, together with his team, were complimented on their considerable achievements, which saw the structure fully converted and back in use after only 27 months.

In the case of the original 1875 lift, the caissons when full of water weighed nominally 252 tons when mounted on a ram (piston). However, when the lift was converted to electric power, the caissons were connected to wire ropes and each balanced by 18 cast iron

counterweights (the weights suspended down the outside of the lift), they as a consequence weighed only a nominal 14 tons each. A number of the weights have been preserved, and can be seen next to the new visitor centre.

Each caisson is 75ft long by 15ft 6in wide, and they are approximately 5ft deep. The tanks were each designed to hold two 72ft long narrow boats of 6ft 6in wide and with a laden depth (below the water) of 4ft, or alternatively a single barge with a width of 13ft.

During preliminary investigations, and prior to launching a restoration bid, British Waterways at first announced that they intended to restore the lift to electrical operation as converted in 1908 by JA Saner. However, in 1997 the company, in consultation with English Heritage, decided to restore the lift to hydraulic operation as designed by Edwin Clark in 1875. Following several surveys and after much consultation, British Waterways was able in March 2000 to announce the commencement of restoration work.

So for the foreseeable future the unique 'Cathedral of the Waterways' was safe, and the facility reopened to boat traffic and visitors on 20 March 2002.

Viewing the boat lift today, the two distinctive structures can still be clearly

Above: The *Edwin Clark* and its load of visitors start a downward journey. Author.

defined. During the 2002 restoration, the massive steel framework and machinery deck was also refurbished but, because of the return to hydraulic power, it is non-functional. In essence, when looking at this Victorian wonder you are viewing not one, but two boat lifts.

The name of the Anderton Boat Lift's designer was celebrated by the present management when they named a vessel (specifically designed for transporting visitors between the river and the canal) in his honour. Trips aboard the *Edwin Clark* have become a popular innovation and they allow the workings of this engineering wonder to be viewed 'close up and personal'.

That great champion of industrial Britain, the late Fred Dibnah, MBE, described his 2004 visit to Anderton as 'simply wonderful' and stated that, of all the many engineering wonders he had in the past examined, he considered the boat lift to be up there with the very best. On a warm summer evening at the end of a filming assignment, Fred took a short trip by traditional narrow boat along the Weaver Navigation and it was something, he said as he disembarked, that he would like to do again. Sadly, that was not to be.

In addition to the boat lift, the riverside regions of Cheshire are rich in industrial heritage with the Salt Museum at Northwich and the Lion Salt Works, situated alongside the Trent and Mersey Canal at Wincham, both offering 'day visitor added value'. The impressive Ellesmere Port Boat Museum is another must-see attraction within easy travelling distance of Anderton.

Details of the boat lift's construction, subsequent conversion and rebuilding are comprehensively described in several publications, two of which are *The Anderton Boat Lift* by David Carden and published by Black Dwarf Publications and the *Guide to the Anderton Boat Lift* by the same author in conjunction with Neil Parkhouse, and the same publisher. Ⓦ

The Anderton Boat Lift and operations centre opening hours:
Easter to September: 10am-5pm, daily (including bank holidays)
October: 10.30am-3.30pm, Wednesday to Sunday
November: 10.30am-3.30pm, Thursday to Sunday
December and January closed.
To enjoy a trip aboard the glass-topped Edwin Clark or a river cruise along the Weaver Navigation, call 01606 786777

Above left: The *Edwin Clark* at the bottom of the lift (river level). Author.

Above right: The western caisson being raised. Note the hydraulic ram. Author.

Anderton and its unique boat lift;
History in pictures

Pictures from The Waterways Trust.

The original hydraulic lift pictured c1900 with a salt platform and chute to the right of the brick chimney. The coal-fired 10hp steam engine associated with the chimney would have powered the accumulator. The accumulator was a means of storing hydraulic energy that eliminated the need for water towers, and the steam engine would be used to keep it constantly primed.

The Weaver Packet *Burmah*, built as a flat in 1875 and converted to steam in 1882, is seen berthed at Winnington on the Weaver Navigation. The nearby sheds are loaded with loose salt awaiting dispatch. A barrowload of salt appears about to be discharged into the vessel. Suspicions are that this may have been a posed photograph, as it is unlikely that a mixed cargo of loose and bagged salt would ever be loaded. Beyond that vessel, salt chutes can be seen, and a small launch belonging to the Salt Union and named *Pacific* passes by.

In this 1950s picture, narrow boats can be seen moored in the canal basin at the top of the lift. Beyond and on the far bank of the Weaver Navigation is part of the Brunner Mond (ICI) chemical works complex. The aqueduct gate on the right of the picture is closed, with the caisson in the raised position, indicating that the western side of the lift is temporarily out of use.

The addition of the pulley wheels, ropes, counterweights and associated steelwork necessary for the conversion to electric operation can clearly be defined straddling (outside and above) the original structure.

By the 1950s, almost all the salt chutes had been removed. Several Weaver Flats can be seen in the basin awaiting cargoes. Above the masts of the flats can be seen a public house favoured by boatmen. Though correctly titled The Stanley Arms, the pub has always been known to generations of boatman and locals as 'The Tip'. That name is probably a reference to the fact that the chutes were loaded in the vicinity of the pub from barrows.

A view of the western side of the original lift (c1900) showing salt-loading chutes in Anderton basin.

Construction work under way during the building of a deck (machinery platform) to carry the pulleys as part of the conversion to electric operation in 1908. Note the steam-powered derrick erected on the wooden scaffolding. The new A-frames needed to support the machinery platform can clearly be seen.

Cast iron headgear, and all the mechanisms being installed on the machinery deck. The bearings for the drive shafts can be seen in the foreground. The workers are most likely installing base plates to accommodate an electric motor and gearbox.

The way it used to be done: A young riveter at work on the Anderton Boat Lift, c1900.

Virtual Waterways
means 60,000 records at your fingertips!

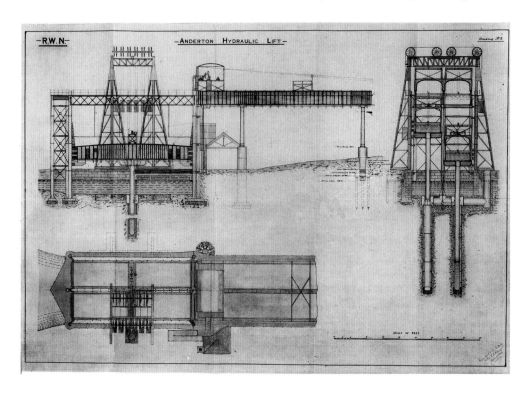

Above: This detailed drawing of the unique 1875 Anderton Boat Lift, as originally built to be hydraulically operated, is representative of many such items within the virtual archive.

Anyone with an interest in our industrial heritage or the evolution of the canal system, or wishing to trace their family tree, will be able to search through more than 60,000 waterways files from the comfort of their own home. The aptly named Virtual Waterways is an ambitious project encapsulating thousands of records, many dating from the 17th century, and spanning to the present day. They have been collated to form an online, easily navigable database that will provide a fascinating new interactive website, guaranteed to become popular in no time at all.

The site www.virtualwaterways.co.uk allows instant access to the waterways archives from any PC connected to the World Wide Web.

This project brings together information from the 15 different locations that make up the British Waterways Archives to one virtual site. This means that previously inaccessible records have now become available, forming a pre-eminent historical resource. Detailed information from the archives can now be researched by anyone from wherever they live, while the actual records are retained in the localities to which they relate.

The collections consist of material relating to British Waterways and its predecessors, the original companies that built and maintained the network of inland waterways throughout England, Scotland and Wales. A small number of records are for waterways outside the United Kingdom, including Ireland.

At present, 163 canal companies are currently listed in the catalogue, including post-nationalisation bodies up to 1970. Types of material held include maps and plans, photographs and documentary material, the bulk of which dates from the middle of the 18th century to the late 20th. The catalogue will enable local access to remotely held information for many diverse topics.

These include the histories of local communities on and around waterways, details of vessels and enhanced family details from canal workers' records, in addition to local environmental and habitat studies of waterways corridors. Heritage and listed building studies are naturally included and the database will also be an invaluable resource for those conducting archaeological investigations. This project was made possible thanks to part-funding from the Heritage Lottery Fund.

ESSENTIAL PROTECTION FOR ALL BOATS & YACHTS

Plug into shore power? You need one NOW!

Galvanic and stray current corrosion can be devastating to any vessel but can easily be controlled by this simple easy D.I.Y. fit device. Every boat should have one!

Galvanic corrosion causes rapid anode loss, prop and shaft damage, skin fitting and engine anode loss and hull damage but can be easily controlled.

Recommended by marine surveyors and now standard fitting on most production boats our low cost galvanic isolators will prevent not only destructive galvanic currents but also control stray currents allowing you to leave shore power connected without the worries of galvanic corrosion.

Don't wait till the surveyor calls with the bad news: protect your investment now!

Our low cost isolators are designed to highest ABYC spec and are compliant to all legislation worldwide. Epoxy sealed, ignition protected and designed for the harsh marine environment. 110 or 240 volts worldwide compatibility.

Free information pack:
Phone: 01977 513607 Fax: 0113 2774797
Email: Galvanic.isolators@virgin.net
Online: Info/help/advice/ordering/technical help:
www.galvanicisolators.com.
Or write to: Safeshore Marine, Millmoor House, Low Common, Methley, Leeds LS26 9AF. Yorkshire.

SAFESHORE MARINE UK

SUPPLIERS OF HIGH QUALITY GALVANIC ISOLATORS TO THE MARINE INDUSTRY

SATELLITE TV
Fitting service at your location
To include cable, connectors and all leads, plus a demonstration showing you how to set up your new system.

From **£75**

Satellite Prices

Sat Finder Kit From **£50**

Satellite Dish From **£125**

LCD & LCD/DVD TV'S
14" LCD TV From **£225**
15" LCD TV From **£250**
17" LCD TV From **£350**
15" LCD/DVD From **£350**
17" LCD/DVD From **£450**
12 VOLT TV'S POA

Digi Box From **£200**

Call Martyn on 07914 401 036

Satellite Packages

PACKAGE 1 From £375.00	• Satellite Dish • Digi Box with own TV • Satellite Finder Kit
PACKAGE 2 From £650.00	• Satellite Dish • Digi Box • 15" LCD TV • Sat Finder Kit
PACKAGE 3 From £725.00	• Satellite Dish • Digi Box • 17" LCD TV • Sat Finder Kit

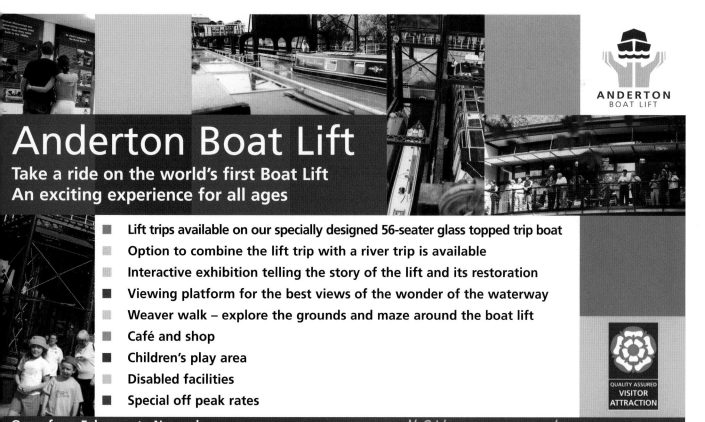

Anderton Boat Lift

Take a ride on the world's first Boat Lift
An exciting experience for all ages

- Lift trips available on our specially designed 56-seater glass topped trip boat
- Option to combine the lift trip with a river trip is available
- Interactive exhibition telling the story of the lift and its restoration
- Viewing platform for the best views of the wonder of the waterway
- Weaver walk – explore the grounds and maze around the boat lift
- Café and shop
- Children's play area
- Disabled facilities
- Special off peak rates

Open from February to November
Lift trips and river trips operating April to October
Group rates available for
groups of 12 or more (Pre booking essential)
■ Charges and terms & conditions apply

ANDERTON BOAT LIFT

QUALITY ASSURED VISITOR ATTRACTION

an uplifting experience
For bookings and information call **01606 786777**
or visit **www.andertonboatlift.co.uk.**

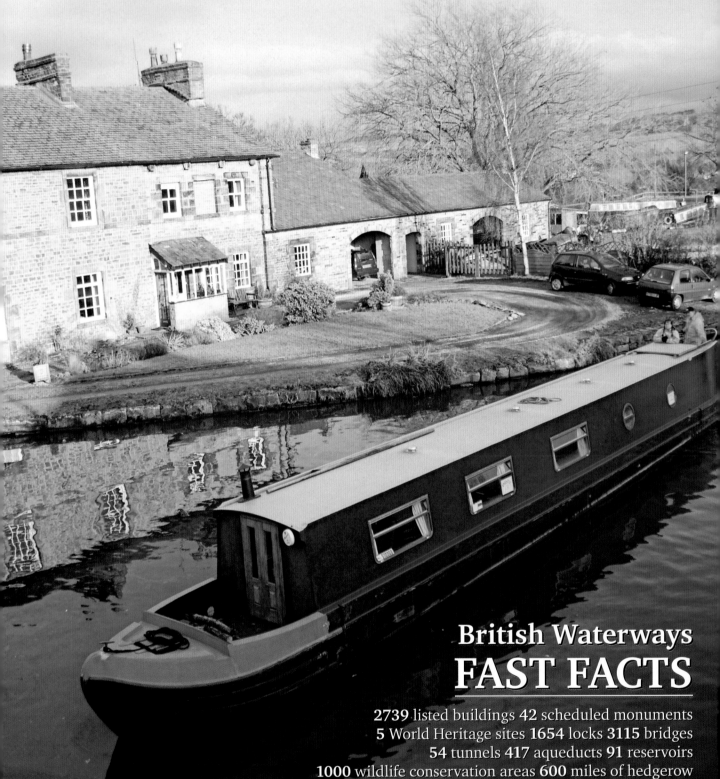

British Waterways

British Waterways
FAST FACTS

2739 listed buildings **42** scheduled monuments
5 World Heritage sites **1654** locks **3115** bridges
54 tunnels **417** aqueducts **91** reservoirs
1000 wildlife conservation areas **600** miles of hedgerow
1000s of archaeological sites **60** Specific Scientific Interest areas
1036 lock cottages and dwellings **8** historic battlefields

British Waterways cares for more than 2000 miles of canals and rivers, two thirds of the UK's total waterways heritage

Britain's
waterways
once forgotten, now cherished

How a major custodian sees the future of the waterways

At its greatest extent in the 18th century, Britain's inland waterway network stretched to over 5000 miles and carried 30-million tonnes of goods and raw materials every year. A criss-cross of watery highways spread like tentacles across England and Wales and from coast to coast in Scotland. Almost all the major cities and towns had a canal, from London to Lancaster and from Wales to the Wash. In a short space of time it became possible to move large cargoes over great distances as the transport system that kick-started the country's Industrial Revolution was built.

Today British Waterways manages over two-thirds of the 3000 miles that remain of the waterway network. A public corporation, they are the largest navigation authority in the UK. An interesting fact is that half the population of the UK live within five miles of one of the nation's canals or rivers.

Working to promote and enhance the canal and river network, British Waterways ensures that some of the country's most important environmental assets, home to a wonderful array of wildlife, are attractive places to visit and are beneficial to society. BW are also charged with caring for the third-largest collection of listed structures in the UK, a diverse heritage estate ranging from 200-year-old locks, bridges, tunnels and aqueducts to simple reminders of the past, such as waterway mileposts and stabling blocks.

Above: Built originally to carry freight, our waterways are a valuable leisure amenity enjoyed and appreciated by many. Author.

Top left: An all-women work boat crew, possibly during the time of conscription (WWII) British Waterways.

Top right: Not all the work to be carried out is easy to see; only after the canal has been drained can this paddle mechanism be properly examined. Author.

Above: Building the canals was dangerous physical work. The Waterways Trust.

A waterways renaissance

Two centuries after the waterways were built to carry cargoes of goods and materials, a small amount of commercial freight continues to ply its trade there. However, today the waterways are primarily a thriving leisure resource. More than 300-million visits each year are made to British Waterways' canals and rivers by walkers, cyclists, anglers, boaters and those simply enjoying a relaxing drink in a waterside cafe/bar or just going along to feed the ducks. Quite simply, people like to live, work and socialise next to water.

Central to the waterways' appeal are the colourful canal boats. Adding activity and vibrancy, the boats provide an insight into bygone days when the waterways were at the heart of industrial Britain. Currently there are more than 26,000 leisure boats on the canals and rivers that BW administer. They are skippered by a rich mixture of experienced enthusiasts and first-time boaters.

The waterways and their hedgerows, towpath verges, grassy embankments and reedy fringes, wind their way through Britain's towns and cities, acting as green arteries in urban corridors. They can be a source of regeneration, transforming rundown, post-industrial urban landscapes and, as such, have been rediscovered as an attractive part of modern living. Waterways are the focal-point of a vibrant renaissance that benefits urban communities and rural economies alike by bringing new life, valuable income and much-needed social inclusion.

Our waterways form an unbroken and freely accessible corridor linking towns, cities and vast areas of open countryside across the United Kingdom. Because of their historic structures, they embrace the character of the past, a quality that attracts millions of visitors every year. The very special and different sense of place and character created by their historic structures is why so many people value and make use of 'their' waterways every day.

Today's vibrant waterways have not always been desirable places in which to relax and unwind. The rapid rise in the construction of canals for freight carriage was less than 50 years

later followed by the beginning of decades of decline as other transport networks came into being. First it was competition for freight traffic from the railways in the 19th century and thereafter motor transport in the 20th. The perhaps inevitable success of those other carriers, coupled with the decline of Britain's traditional industries, led to many miles of waterways being abandoned or isolated. In short, the integrated system began to disintegrate.

Communities that had once embraced the waterways turned their back on the network, and many miles of canal became unattractive no-go areas. New housing and road transport developments led to a great deal of building over the redundant waterways and severed not only the water highways themselves but also the communities that had grown up to provide for and work on 'the cut'. The gradual but inevitable decline took place on a national scale.

After WWII long-term underfunding became a way of life for the waterways. With no perceived need to invest in a transport network that was outdated, and without the vision to realise the potential of the waterways for leisure and recreation opportunities, successive governments provided a series of shoestring budgets for their maintenance.

However, the tireless work of bands of willing volunteers and a few enlightened local authorities led to the first signs of people realising that not all of this relic from the Industrial Revolution would be lost, supposedly in the name of 'progress'. Very gradually the tide turned towards acknowledging and unlocking the potential of the remaining network for a hugely varied number of uses.

By the mid-1990s, British Waterways and a selection of partners were successfully making the case for increased investment in the network. Pioneering regeneration and waterway restoration schemes began to demonstrate the economic, social and environmental potential that revitalised waterways could deliver. New funds from the European Union, development agencies and the national lottery – particularly the Millennium Commission and the Heritage Lottery Fund - unlocked many restoration projects that had

Above: The fantastic Neptune's Stair Case locks at Banavie, near Fort William, are situated on the Caledonian Canal.
© james Gentles 2004.

Top left: Much of the trade on the bigger rivers in the late 19th and early 20th centuries was plied by schooners and other sailing boats. Rick Ferris Archive.

Top right: 21st century canal-side cityscape, Oozells Street loop in modern Birmingham. Author.

Above left: Most of the increase in visitor numbers will be in urban areas, so there will always be the countryside peace and tranquillity that is an important part of the waterways' appeal, for those who seek to find it. Author.

Above right: Carrying out essential repairs c1900. The Waterways Trust.

long been spoken of as desirable but until that time had remained unrealised.

Possibly the most significant breakthrough came in February 1999, when the then Government announced new support and money for British Waterways after decades of underfunding. Add into that equation the products of half-a-century of campaigning by dedicated volunteers and enthusiasts, and more than 150 years of decline was beginning to be rectified. Those combined efforts saw the waterway network at last begin to expand and thrive.

In 2006 BW, along with their restoration partners, will start works valued at more than £60-million. Projects include the Liverpool Canal Link, which will connect Liverpool's world-famous docks with the Leeds & Liverpool Canal; and the Droitwich Canals, which were once a gateway from the industrial heartlands of the Black Country to the rest of the world. The first phase of the restoration of the Cotswolds Canals, which on completion will link the River Thames in the east with the

Gloucester & Sharpness Canal in the west, is now under way.

The arrival in 2012 of the London Olympic Games provides an unparalleled opportunity to transform the derelict Bow Back Rivers area of London. These magnificent restoration and new-build projects, along with the many more spearheaded by canal societies and enthusiasts across the country, will hopefully ensure that the waterways continue to expand, thrive and serve all sections of the community.

British Waterways is not directly funded solely and specifically to deliver any of the particular schemes mentioned. To that end, they have to work hard to encourage others to provide the necessary extra funds. Among the bodies they work with are the HLF, local authorities and a multiplicity of other third-party funders, including sources originating in Europe. It is now unquestionably accepted that revived waterways deliver significant economic, social and environmental benefits that are judged to be way beyond the actual cost of restoration.

200 years of working history

Pioneering engineers were the heroes of the canal age, building structures never attempted before. Waterways were carried across valleys on high aqueducts, climbed slopes by means of ingenious inclined planes or flights of locks, and were conveyed straight through hills in deep, dark tunnels which, during their construction, claimed many workers' lives. Those engineers presented Britain with a very valuable heritage legacy.

In addition to its listed structures, British Waterways' treasure trove includes 42 scheduled monuments (some of which are whole lengths of canal), 311 miles (500km) of conservation areas and thousands of archaeological sites. In addition, the waterways under their control adjoin or bisect five World Heritage sites, eight historic battlefields and 12 registered historic parks.

Running a 200-year-old waterway is, in effect, like looking after a historically important and valuable asset, but in reality one that isn't locked-up in a museum but is in day-to-day use. That function brings with it some unique challenges. To ensure that the heritage is cared for correctly,

British Waterways employs dedicated heritage professionals who advise on the care and upkeep of the waterways. The correct conservation materials and techniques that need to be used are vital if future generations are to be allowed to enjoy and value the waterways network as we do now at the beginning of the 21st century.

In addition there is a very significant number of canal enthusiasts and volunteers who support the work done by British Waterways and thus help safeguard the heritage through their own commitment. The vast majority of the nation's fleet of historic canal boats are owned by enthusiasts. They embrace basic technology and graceful lines when restoring their craft much in the same way as, for instance, those who look after classic motor vehicles. The challenge is to make those wonderful craft work today as well as they did when they first plied the system. There are the thriving historic narrow boat owners' clubs, canal restoration societies, a horse boating society, friends of canal museums and other supportive organisations all prepared to

Top left: Old ways, old crafts: a boatman is seen making a rope fender. The Waterways Trust.

Top right: Britain's inland waterway network at one time stretched over 5000 miles and carried 30-million tonnes of goods and raw materials every year. British Waterways.

Left: To check on canal and reservoir levels, BW have a state-of-the-art monitoring system called Scada. This is the picturesque Whitemoor Reservoir. British Waterways.

contribute, with passion, to all aspects of the waterways scene.

The most impressive and outstanding heritage structures and buildings are well protected and British Waterways will always find the funds to keep them in good order. However, it is the smaller features like old lock winding gear, strapping posts, stables and rubbing strips that cause the greatest concern. Although small, they add hugely to the interest, character and history of the waterways. They help visitors interpret a given area and relate the canals to the local community. Ensuring that these qualities are not lost, or that improvements to the system do not marginalise them, is a constant balancing act that BW strives hard to

manage almost on a day-to-day basis.

The 'as-built' heritage of our waterways is the key essential ingredient that makes them so attractive and popular. British Waterways are very conscious of the need to work exceptionally hard in order to keep alive the unique history and culture of the waterways system. Proper care and thoughtful preservation will ensure their futures. But the pressures are enormous, as developers increasingly want to rebuild and reshape the land and buildings around the waterways.

As part of the drive to manage the heritage of the waterways successfully, BW is developing a series of heritage partnership agreements for key historic sites. These agreements are being

Top left: Keeping the boat traffic moving means carrying out constant maintenance, both planned and emergency. This is dredging under way on the Grand Union Canal. British Waterways.

Top right: Freight being loaded into river boats at the Winnington ICI works in the 1950s. Fick Ferris Archive.

Right: Canal-side public houses – a very old and well-liked tradition. This is the Kings Lock pub on the Trent & Mersey Canal in Middlewich. Author.

piloted ahead of the new heritage protection regime and will permit greater self-regulation and accountability. This approach by BW is seen as 'right for the waterways' and, in the ground-breaking venture, they are working closely with English Heritage, various local authorities and several other stakeholders in order to achieve their stated aims.

Another 200 years of history

It is an expensive business looking after a 200-year-old working waterway network. Each year British Waterways spend well over £100-million on core maintenance. That figure includes dredging the channels of the canals, repairing lock gates, bridges and other historic structures and, of course, more routine tasks like cutting back vegetation along the many miles of towpaths.

The long-term funding of the waterways is a critical issue and the majority of the population feel that never again should the prosperity of the waterways be subject to the vagaries of government funding, as it was in the last century.

BW's objective is for society to fully appreciate the value of the waterways so that they rightly take their place alongside royal palaces, the coastline and national parks as some of the nation's most treasured national assets. Ensuring that the current Government supports the waterways is a priority.

However, at the same time they are looking

Top left: The way it was: bulk salt is loaded down a chute (from the canal above) to this river steamer on the Weaver Navigation. Ellesmere Port Boat Museum.

Top right: The objective British Waterways has firmly in its sights is to ensure that the waterways many cherish today will still be available for future generations to enjoy tomorrow. Author.

Left: British Waterways is anxious to tackle what it sees as a dire shortage of berthing facilities by encouraging the construction of new marinas like this one at Burton Water on the Witham Navigation. Author.

Top left: Some work BW has to carry out is very avoidable. If only all people respected the canals and stopped ill-treating them! Supermarket trolley recovery on the Staffordshire & Worcester canal. British Waterways.

Top right: Coal made up a big part of the total cargo tonnages originally carried by narrow boats. The Waterways Trust.

Bottom right: BW has more than 90 reservoirs to maintain. This is work under way at Knypersley in Staffordshire. It is a picturesque 40-acre reservoir located within Greenway Bank Country Park. British Waterways.

at ways in which the 18th century canal and river systems can fit in with the day-to-day requirements of the 21st century. Built originally to facilitate commerce and therefore to make money, today's waterways should be no different. British Waterways' vision for the future includes the system becoming largely financially self-sufficient in the long term.

Undoubtedly the primary use of the waterways today is no longer freight but predominantly leisure and tourism. Accordingly BW has plans to double the number of visitors to the vast and utilitarian amenity that is the modern system. Most of the increase in visitor numbers will be in urban areas, so there will always be the countryside peace and tranquillity that is an important part of the waterways' appeal for those who seek to find it. The corporation state that they are constantly looking at other innovative ventures to increase the total of revenue generated.

British Waterways is, of course, pledged to grow the income it receives from leisure and

tourism. Boat owners pay to keep their boats on the waterways, and BW also earns good annual income from angling. In the last few years earnings have been complemented by some new revenue streams such as canal visitor centres and waterside cafes. Just for good measure and definitely in the true British spirit (no puns intended), British Waterways now have an interest in a network of waterside pubs!

All the money that British Waterways earns from whatever sources is reinvested into the care and upkeep of the waterways. They recognise that it is the responsibility of this generation to look after the inheritance due to future generations, so that they may be able to appreciate the national system and, in turn, learn what a great part those waterways played in shaping Britain's industrial heritage. The objective British Waterways has firmly in its sights is to ensure that the waterways many cherish today will still be available for future generations to enjoy tomorrow. **w**

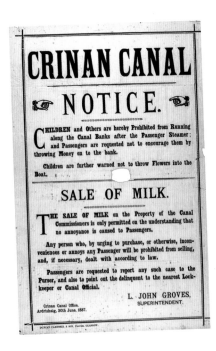

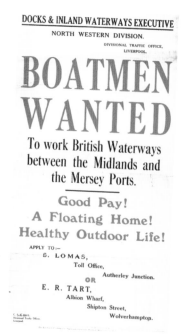

Gas Street Basin on the Birmingham Main Line, where ancient meets modern in a big way. Author.

The Weaver Navigation

Winsford to Runcorn through the heart of Cheshire – opened 1732

The river on which salt was king

There are many rivers, estuaries and creeks throughout the British Isles that were once very busy waterways and upon which many of the local population depended for their living. The revolutionary Anderton Boat Lift was a successful concept primarily because it was built at the right time and very definitely in the right place. As a snapshot of that lost way of life we highlight the Weaver Navigation.

The Brunner Mond Company (later to become Imperial Chemical Industries) had established itself in mid-Cheshire – a location rich in a mineral that all the world's developing industrial nations would come to rely on in one way or another. As coal was king in many parts of Britain so salt was king in Cheshire.

In deed salt had been mined in the Northwich Area since Roman Times. Brunner Mond Ltd used brine drawn from the vast underground salt deposits in their chemical processes and, at the end of that cycle, they moved their finished goods using the river. Their products were distributed worldwide by their own fleet of Weaver river boats that plied to the docks in Liverpool.

From the 1950s they also moved product by 'coasters', both their own and contracted vessels. That busy trade was, of course, in addition to the traditional salt-for-consumption trade carried out in the region by a whole host of other companies. The 'lift' made easier (and less labour-intensive so more economical) the connection and therefore the movement of cargo between the Trent & Mersey Canal and the Weaver Navigation.

Above: The preserved ex-ICI river boat *Davenham* is pictured at Dutton Locks. Clive Guthrie.

The River Weaver rises beyond Nantwich, in south Cheshire, and passes through the towns of Winsford and Northwich before skirting Frodsham on its passage to the sea which, in earlier times, it entered via the Mersey estuary. Nowadays the river joins the Manchester Ship Canal, close to Weston Point Docks near Runcorn, before entering the Mersey via a suitable set of sea locks.

The Weaver was at that time tidal, which made access difficult, and even then only allowed barges to travel some six miles inland. Consequently, in 1663 the desirability of increasing the navigation from Frodsham to Winsford (20 miles upstream), thus being able to take advantage of revenue generated by the salt trade, was discussed. But it was not until 1721 that an Act of Parliament, allowing the construction to begin, was passed, with the building of the 'navvy' being completed in 1732.

Over the following 250 years it was steadily improved, being deepened and widened, and benefiting from the addition of five sets of locks. It became a very important local trade route carrying not only salt but china clay, flint and finished ceramic products.

In 1777 trade on the Weaver fell sharply, following the opening of the Trent & Mersey Canal, a section of which traverses the same valley as the Weaver, as does the smaller and unnavigable River Dane. The canal being built on the higher northern bank of the Dane Valley skirted Northwich, approximately 60ft (18.2 metres) above the Weaver at Anderton.

The trustees of the Weaver Navigation, at first shocked by the sudden loss of trade, were then galvanised into activity by the very existence of the canal and responded by constructing the Anderton Basin which, in modern terms, would be called a 'freight interchange depot'. A tramway was built in 1799 and, by the turn of the century, salt chutes had been constructed, all of which led to a successful and anticipated increase in river trade.

Now, instead of competing, the two organisations were working together in order to allow goods carried from inland areas by narrow boat to be transferred to larger vessels on the river and thence to docks on the Mersey, mainly in the vicinity of Liverpool. While the interchange was without doubt successful it was, of course, a one-way operation and was severely limited in capacity.

The traditional River Weaver boats, or barges, were known as 'Weaver Flats' and the men who worked them were accordingly referred to as 'flatmen'. The records for the year 1817 show that there were in the region of 5000 men regularly 'working' between 300 and 500 boats. It was a hard life for small reward, a fact I have heard stated on many occasions as my late grandfather, Joe Deakin, was a Northwich born 'flatman'.

By 1885 there were said to be 265 craft, of which 65 were steam powered, plying their trade on the navigation with upwards of 100 sailings weekly in each direction. These vessels carried one-million tonnes of salt and 300,000 tonnes of china clay and potters' materials between them each year.

That the Weaver Navigation owed almost all of its commercial success to the local salt and chemical industry is without doubt, and the navigation played a big part in creating wealth in the area, particularly in the salt towns of Northwich and Winsford. However, the area paid a high price for that wealth with the water quality in those unenlightened times becoming extremely poor as pollution from the riverside industries took place in an almost unchecked manner.

In post-WWII years, the pollution problems were tackled in earnest and coupled with new

Above left: The Weaver is now popular with walkers, anglers and boaters. This is the stretch between New Bridge at Meadow Bank and Vale Royal locks looking downstream. Author.

Above right: 1950s night shift at Wallerscote Quay on the Weaver Navigation.
Rick Ferris Collection.

and cleaner production methods being introduced by the riverside industrial units, the Weaver began to return to a more natural state. As the industries began to decline and shrink, commercial river traffic came almost completely to an end.

The Northwich ship building companies of WJ Yarwood & Sons and Issac Pimblott (Pimblotts of Northwich), which built coasters, river boats, tugs, canal craft and even motor torpedo boats, ceased to trade. It had been a great treat for the youngsters of the area to be allowed out of school to watch a launching, as both yards often achieved this feat by presenting the craft to the river in a 'sideways' aspect the displacement of which created an impressive splash.

Pimblotts yard above Hunts Lock is now a privately owed boatyard and marina, as is the ex-BW narrow boat repair facility in the Northwich Town Basin. Sadly the British Waterways repair yard that stood close to the old Yarwoods shipyard has also closed and, while no plans have been announced that would secure its riverside usefulness as a repair facility, neither have plans been made public yet concerning its conversion to riverside dwellings. But, as they say, watch this space!

Today the river and its valley provide a host of recreational opportunities including boating, walking, rowing, canoeing and fishing. The Weaver Valley landscape is distinctive and the undisturbed sections include old river channels, ancient woodland and wet meadows that have significant nature conservation interest. These make an important contribution to the landscape and nature of the valley and enhance its worth as a waterside public amenity.

Over the past two or three years the Weaver Valley between Winsford and Northwich has been turned into a delightful linear country park. The reclamation of former chemical production and salt mining areas in and around the towns of Northwich and Winsford has created important wildlife habitats, and new networks of cycle and bridleways have been introduced. The Weaver Navigation is kept well dredged and its availability to boaters from all over the national network has been made much easier by the reopening of Anderton Boat Lift.

The modern cut has four sets of locks and five swing bridges, of which the single-track Newbridge installation next to Winsford Rock Salt Mine is the least impressive, followed closely by the low swing bridge at Winnington, which is suitable only for single-line road traffic and thus controlled by traffic lights. The matching pair of

Above: February 1946, and Northwich town centre under water. Note the two swing bridges (Town Bridge at the top left) are seen either side of the Town Basin. The former BW repair yard is seen bottom centre, with the Liverpool Lighterage Company's dock opposite. The current BW Wales & Border Counties regional offices are still located in the buildings next to the clock tower just below Hayhurst Bridge on Navigation Road. The River Dane flows into the Weaver just in front of the gas holder (now dismantled). Archive.

Top left: Picnic time for this flotilla of narrow boats that have just come up Vale Royal locks. Author

Top right: Where salt was king – an ICI manager looks at the river traffic, c1960. Rick Ferris collection.

Below left: The former Pimblotts boatyard above Hunts lock, Northwich. Author.

Below right: Two narrow boats alongside the coaster *Tora* in Anderton Basin c1965. Clive Guthrie.

floating pontoon type bridges guarding either side of the town centre in Northwich are without doubt the most interesting.

They are the Hayhurst Bridge (1898) and Town Bridge (1899). Both are wonders of the Victorian age and as such are rightly Grade II-listed buildings. They were the first of their type to be built and are also said to be the first electrically powered swing bridges constructed in Britain. There are two more modern but equally impressive swing bridges over the navigation: Acton Swing Bridge, which carries the A49, and Sutton Swing Bridge, near Frodsham, which carries the A56.

During the winter months of 2005-6, British Waterways invested £450,000 in a major dredging programme along the Weaver Navigation removing silt deposits causing an obstruction to boating traffic. Keeping the water flowing is also important as, in the past, the town centre of Northwich has been seriously affected by flooding.

The Environment Agency carries this stark but nevertheless informative note on its website: 'Northwich lies where the rivers Dane and Weaver meet and, at times of high flows, the rivers can overtop their banks. This, combined with the fact that the town has suffered from subsidence because of years of salt mining, means the area is at risk of flooding.'

Flooding has fortunately in modern times not reached the severity the events of February 1946 when exceptional rainfall locally, and in the foothills of Pennines where the River Dane rises, caused the whole of the town centre to be submerged under several feet of water. The River Weaver, already at a high level, was unable to cope with the added volume of River Dane water forced into it at their confluence, an area known locally as Dane Bridge. The result was a predictable disaster for the town.

To help keep the river flowing and also deep enough to allow the passage of craft (now set at a minimum depth of three metres) dredging of the river just below its confluence with the Dane has always been necessary. That section of river just downstream of the Town Bridge is referred to as Barons Quay.

On its way through mid-Cheshire the River Dane meanders through pleasant farm land and many changes in its course have taken place. The Dane's speed of flow when flushed with Pennine rainwater can be awesome to behold. As the river gains strength it washes away hundreds of tons of soil with a high sharp sand content from the banks that keep it within the surrounding meadowlands.

Upon reaching Northwich, the river is forced into a narrower section where it then 'at a rush' joins the River Weaver. It has in suspension the solids carved from its banks, which are then swept along with the Weaver's own water under the Town Bridge, another narrowing point which further accelerates the flow and helps to keeps the solids suspended. A few yards farther downstream the Weaver widens considerably and, in doing so, its rate of flow reduces noticeably. That action allows the sand and soil being carried in the water to be released from suspension, and it naturally falls to the river bed.

Two types of dredging were used on the recent Weaver Navigation work – hopper boat dredging around Baron's Quay and Saltersford Locks and suction dredging using a high pressure pipeline system around Dutton Locks. They have in principle the same aim but in practice are so different from the old method. In the 1960s I took a summer vacation job with British Waterways and worked, albeit briefly, with a dredging crew aboard a steam-powered hopper boat.

There were two mud boats (hoppers) working in turn from a clanking old bucket dredger named *Witton* as it traversed the width of the river adjacent to Barons Quay. I am sure that the 'hoppers' were called alternatively *Shark* and *Whale* and I believe that the latter was the steam vessel I worked on. The other 'slutch boat' was a then-new (to BW) diesel-powered craft.

The method was that we faced upstream and alongside the dredger while the buckets employed by that vessel emptied the dredge, via a chute, into our hold. When full, or when the skipper was fed up (and the two were never the same thing), we would head off with our cargo.

On this particular job our voyage was a long one as the spoil was being settled into a lagoon above Hunts Lock and near Hartford Stone

Bridge. I think we made two round-trips a day. The sides of the steam hopper boat were flotation chambers so that, when we reached our appointed discharge point, we would release chains fixed in pulleys that, in turn, allowed two doors in the bottom of the hull to open (downwards), the spoil then falling to the river bed. The old steamer would then pop up just like a cork, having lost the weight of her cargo.

We would set back slowly away from the drop zone and a steam winch would noisily haul the underwater doors back into place. I remembered thinking at the time 'all very hidden, one-man submarine stuff' – well, schoolboys did dream!

The dredge, which we had, in this instance, conveyed some two miles, was then the problem of the crew on the 'sucker boat'. That craft would 'lift' the silt using its suction pump and blow it up the bank into the settlement lagoons. That is what the modern-day suction dredger does, but it, of course, cuts out the middle man!

Of course, now the clanking bucket dredger is gone; instead there is a huge mechanical shovel on a floating pontoon. In use on the recent dredge of Barons Quay were two unpowered hopper boats, one at each end of the silt operation. The empty one is held firmly against the floating pontoon and is during that time accompanied by a tug under power and facing upstream, while the shovel engages with the river bottom and quickly fills the hopper with sand etc.

As this activity is under way, the second barge is being unloaded by a mechanical shovel of similar proportions a little way downstream. The tug will then swap over the barges as required. In this safety-conscious age there is quite rightly another vessel in attendance, a safety boat that doubles as a more-than-adequate floating mess room and toilet facility.

Above left: A 1960s picture of one of the ICI's own coasters, *Polythene,* seen on the Clyde in Glasgow. Rick Ferris Collection.

Above right: 1960s line-up at Winnington that includes a coaster, seen farthest from the camera. Rick Ferris collection.

The modern suction method of dredging had been completed on this section of the river during my visit. In fact the machine, which breaks down into eight sections for road transportation, was being readied for relocation. This is some piece of kit and it can, if needs be (with the help of a boaster station), push 12in of silt an incredible two-and-a-half miles. Built and owned by Humber Work Boats the 11-year-old *John M* is a 1.2m draft, 35m long craft operated by two men.

Other differences from 1960-something? Firstly, the working conditions of the dredge crews, none of whom are direct BW employees, and their support team leave nothing to be desired. The attention to detail and use of only safe working practices is very obviously the first and most important consideration of British Waterways, their surveyors ADAS, dredging experts Blue Boar Contracts Ltd and their contracted team of watermen. No directly owned BW river craft were in use and the tug *Northwich* (ex BW) and safety boat *Conveyor* were provided on contract by Weaver Valley Cruising of Acton Bridge.

The present-day river ceases to be navigable, for all but the smallest craft after reaching Winsford, where any upstream journey necessitates the negotiation of two shallow but picturesque lakes referred to locally as the Bottom and Top Flash. In addition to the section known as Winsford Flashes, the course of the old river is still easily traceable, particularly around Northwich, and Frodsham.

Alternatively, the fascination of the Weaver Navigation can be enjoyed by taking a well defined walk along the towpath between Winsford and Northwich. Signs of the modern-day salt industry can be seen including the rock salt stockpiles at the UK's only working salt mine, next to the hamlet of Meadow Bank. Midway between the towns at Vale Royal, a good example of a Victorian lock system, still in use but in need of extensive renovation, can be examined exclusively by the walker or boater as it is in a truly rural setting, there being no public road access to the lock.

In addition to the 'boat lift', this area of mid-Cheshire is rich in industrial heritage with the Salt Museum at Northwich and the Lion Salt Works, situated alongside the Trent & Mersey Canal at Wincham, both offering 'day visitor added value'.

The impressive Ellesmere Port Boat Museum is another must-see attraction within easy travelling distance of Anderton. **W**

Top left: Loading at Winnington Quay opposite the Anderton Boat Lift. Rick Ferris Collection.

Top right: A current view of the Anderton Boat Lift and the former ICI chemical works either side of the Weaver looking downstream. Author.

Right: Dredging the Weaver at Barons Quay, Northwich, 2006-style. Author.

Boat launch Northwich-style

The Imperial Chemical Industries river boat 'Wincham' is launched side ways at the former river Weaver shipyard of W J Yarwood & Sons Northwich

Pictures from the Rick Ferris Collection.

The chosen few

As their restorations draw to a close, **Alan Barnes** reviews the 10 historically different but important working canal boats that were lucky enough to be selected for restoration in the lottery-funded British Waterways Working Boats Project.

Main: Star Class boats *Leo* and *Atlas* on show in Birmingham in 2005. Neil Howes

Above left: New lining style and cabin exterior for Carina a year later in 2004. Neil Howes

While the heyday of commercial goods-carrying traffic on our inland waterways is but a distant memory, there are one or two schemes in operation that have seen cargo boats return to some waterways.

Generations of boatmen and their families were once responsible for moving huge amounts of goods and raw materials up and down the UK. The coming of the railways heralded the decline of canal traffic and, over the years, thousands of working boats and barges were scrapped or just left to rot in some quiet backwater.

We are fortunate that, thanks largely to the activities of individuals and volunteer groups, some of these historic craft have been saved and many restored. And they're probably cleaner and in mechanically better condition than when they were, for example, plying the Grand Union Canal taking loads of coal into London.

However, some important examples of working boats were still in danger of being lost and it was with this in mind that British Waterways initiated their Working Boats Project (WBP), which identified 10 different boats for preservation and possible restoration.

Funding was required but money alone wasn't the answer. Specialist craftsmen would need to be involved, to work alongside the researchers and volunteers – all making a major contribution.

Work on each of the boats would be photographed and filmed, while archives would be searched for documentation and photographs to trace the history of each boat.

Work on the project began in 2000 and was completed this year at a cost of almost £500,000, with 64 per cent of the funding coming from the Heritage Lottery Memorial Fund.

Not only would the project restore the working boats, it would also create volunteer teams to operate them on various waterways, where they would be part of an education programme for schools and interested groups covering all aspects of canals, boats and canal life.

The selection of the 10 boats for the project would include examples of the traditional motor boat as well as more mundane, low-profile but nonetheless necessary craft such as the unpowered butty and joey boats.

The joey boats are best described as 'canal barges', and many thousands were at work around the Midlands' canals, primarily for

Atlas being craned back into the water after having her bottom blackened at Alvechurch boatyard in 2005. Neil Howes

moving coal and raw materials. Several joey boats would be towed by the powered narrow boats and, as journeys were usually fairly short, the majority of the joeys weren't fitted with a cabin or crew accommodation, although some featured a very basic shelter. Very few have survived but one example was saved by the WBP and can once again be seen on canals in the Birmingham area.

An example of the joey boat was one of the four boats worked on during the project by Ian Kemp and team at Dadfords Wharf in Stourbridge. The others were *Malus*, *Carina* and *Leo*.

The unpowered butty *Malus* was built in 1935 for the Grand Union Canal Carrying Co (GUCCC) and entered service paired with the *Scorpio*, which is also part of the Working Boats Project. *Malus* entered service with British Waterways following nationalisation of the canal system in January 1948 and was eventually retired from the carrying fleet. It was then transferred to the British Waterways maintenance division and continued in service until the 1990s.

During the 1980s *Malus* spent time on the Worcester & Birmingham Canal moving lock gates and during this period her riveted cabin was removed and replaced with a longer welded

Above: This 1950s British Waterways maintenance fleet piling rig is now on display at Hatton Locks. Simon V Hopkins

Right: Ian Kemp signwrites *Atlas* at Icknield Port Dock in 2004. Neil Howes

'THE LUCKY TEN' WORKING BOATS

Boat: Atlas
Type: Small Woolwich Motor Boat – Star Class
Builder: Harland & Wolff, Woolwich
Date: November 1935
Owner: Grand Union Canal Carrying Company (GUCCC)
Length: 71ft
Beam: 7ft 0½in
Draught: 3ft 6in

Boat: Carina
Type: Small Northwich Butty
Builder: Yarwoods of Northwich
Date: 1935
Owner: GUCCC
Length: 71ft 6in
Beam: 7ft 0½in
Draught: 3ft 3in

Boat: Leo
Type: Small Northwich Butty-Star Class
Builder: Yarwoods of Northwich
Date: 1935
Owner: GUCCC
Length: 71ft 6in
Beam: 7ft 0½in
Draught: 3ft 3in

Boat: Malus
Type: Small Northwich Butty
Builder: Yarwoods of Northwich
Date: 1935
Owner: GUCCC
Length: 71ft 6in
Beam: 7ft 0½in
Draught: 3ft 3in

Boat: Sagitta
Type: Small Northwich Motor Boat – Star Class
Builder: Yarwoods of Northwich
Date: June 1935
Owner: GUCCC
Length: 71ft
Beam: 7ft 0½in
Draught: 3ft 6in

Boat: Scorpio
Type: Small Northwich Motor Boat-Star Class
Builder: Yarwoods of Northwich
Date: October 1935
Owner: GUCCC
Length: 71ft
Beam: 7ft 0½in
Draught: 3ft 6in

Boat: Piling Rig
Built: 1950s
Owner: British Waterways Maintenance fleet piling rig

Boat: Joey Boat
One of the few surviving cargo barges used in coal traffic

Boat: Birmingham
Type: Canal Tug
Builder: Abdela & Mitchell
Date: 1912
Owner: Gloucester & Sharpness New Docks Co. Will form part of permanent display at Tardebigge Maintenance Yard

Boat: Nansen II
Type: Canal Tug
Built: 1951
Owner: British Waterways
Restored as a British Waterways Birmingham Canal Navigation Tug.

Above: The relaunch of *Scorpio*, with *Malus*, at Hatton in March 2005. Neil Howes

Sagitta **in original paint at Birmingham, prior to journeying to Icknield Port for paintwork.** Neil Howes

Below: Lucy Tucker in costume to film Topcloth and Tippet on *Atlas* in June 2002.

version. This work was completed by Stoke-on-Trent Boat Builders, which also fitted a new bottom although, unlike many other butties, she was never converted to a motor boat and has retained her original framework and structure.

The extensive restoration at Ian's yard included the fitting of a new riveted cabin, keelson, welldeck lid and shutt flooring to more accurately reflect her as-built condition. However, certain features that evolved in the following years have been retained to show some of the developments that took place on the carrying boats.

The *Carina* is currently still at Ian's yard, having had extensive work carried out to her hull, and has now been refloated. Work on the cabin is yet to be completed. A sister butty to *Leo*, she was built in 1935 and entered GUCCC service as No 249 and eventually became part of the British Waterways fleet, where she was based at Bull's Bridge with the South Eastern Division Carrying Fleet. In addition to the Grand Union, this fleet also worked the Oxford, Worcester & Birmingham, Coventry and Stratford Canals.

The carrying fleet was disbanded in 1962 and the *Carina* was taken to the Wendover Arm of the Grand Union Canal, where unwanted boats were sunk in the canal. However, *Carina* didn't suffer the watery fate of many of her sisters and was used by Doug and Anita Lear for their Magic Lantern Theatre Show. In the mid-80s she was still in use with the Rainbow Theatre Co until passing into the ownership of Mr and Mrs Prettiman, who sold her back to British Waterways in 1998. She was paired with the motor boat *Sagitta* and used for schools education as floating classrooms around Staffordshire.

In 2002 she was moved to Lapworth, where repair work was undertaken by volunteers who also returned her to the handsome blue and yellow British Waterways livery as used following nationalisation. She was moved to Ian's yard to be rebottomed and for the keelson to be replaced.

Work on the *Leo* was completed in 2001 and she has been finished in the distinctive BW blue and yellow livery. Like the *Malus*, she was built in 1935 by Yarwoods of Northwich for the Grand Union Canal Carrying Co, and was part of an order for 12 pairs of boats. Named after the celestial body, *Leo* is a 'Star' Class butty – commonly known as a Small Northwich Butty – and upon completion was given a Brentford public health registration No 535 and GUCCC fleet No 300.

Originally painted white and two shades of blue, the unpowered butty was recorded as having been paired with the motor boat *Eridanus*, although this pairing would not have been permanent. The restoration retained as much of the original structure as possible and traditional materials and construction methods were also used in the rebuilding. *Leo* has been fitted out as a typical family boat of the 1950s and provides a floating educational resource centre to give visitors an idea of living and working conditions experienced 'on the cut'.

The *Atlas* is an example of a Small Woolwich Motor Boat and was built in 1935 by Harland & Wolff Ltd in Woolwich. Operated originally by the GUCCC as their fleet No 565, she entered service paired with the butty *Atlanta*. The GUCCC livery at that time was the aforementioned 'white and two blues' but this changed in 1937 when the fleet colours became red, white and blue for the coronation of King George VI. These colours were carried until nationalisation, when she was turned out in standard BW blue and yellow. *Atlas* was to remain in service firstly as part of the carrying fleet and then later in the maintenance division working around Birmingham and the Black Country. Now restored, *Atlas* is fitted out as a typical family boat of the 1950s and plays an important educational role.

Maintenance was vital to keep the canal network open and it's a great pity that many of the more specialised maintenance craft have been lost over the years. Piling rigs were used to drive

Above left: *Sagitta* resplendent in her new BW colours in 2005.
Neil Howes

Above right: Restored as a British Waterways Birmingham Canal Navigation tug of 1951, *Nansen II* is seen at Bradley in October 2000.

Below left: In December 2004 the restored *Malus* as a complete craft, including interior decoration.

Below centre: *Malus* of 1935 in dry dock at Tardebigge in July 2002, showing the shape of the existing cabin.

Below right: The 1935 small Northwich butty Carina in dry dock at Hatton in August 2003.
Neil Howes

piles into the canal banks, their flat-bottomed design allowing them to get close to the edge of the canal. An example of this type of boat can be seen at Hatton and was originally used on the Coventry and Ashby Canals. It was acquired by British Waterways' Ocker Hill Maintenance Depot and would have been used by piling gangs.

The *Birmingham* is the oldest boat in the project and is a canal tug of 1912, built by Abdela and Mitchell for the Sharpness New Docks Co. She is the sister boat to *Worcester*. Designed to replace earlier steam tugs, which towed boats through the tunnels near Tardebigge, the new diesel-engined tugs found themselves also being used for general towing and ice-breaking. In 1917 *Birmingham* was sold to Marylebone Council, renamed *Tyburn* and was used to tow rubbish barges along Regents Canal. The boat remained in the south-east, being used variously as a hire boat and a school trip boat until acquisition by British Waterways in the 1990s. The existing structure of *Birmingham* has been preserved and the boat will be part of an interpretative education display at the site of the Tardebigge Maintenance Yard.

Like Birmingham, the *Nansen II* is also a tug but of a much later design and has now been restored as a Birmingham Canal Navigation Tug. Built in 1951 to replace the *Nansen I*, this tug was used on the River Severn and was originally fitted with a wheelhouse to aid navigation on the tidal river. It was acquired by BW for use on the Wyreley & Essington Canal during the 1970s and the wheelhouse was removed and a tiller fitted. The tug was used primarily for moving maintenance

craft around the Birmingham canals and for rubbish clearance.

The final two boats in the project, *Sagitta* and *Scorpio*, were both built in 1935 by Yarwoods and are examples of the Small Northwich Motor Boat.

Following nationalisation, *Sagitta* was used by a Mr and Mrs Littler, who lived aboard the boat and carried goods for BW on the Staffs & Worcester and the Trent and Mersey Canals. Towards the end of the 1960s they gave up the boat and it became part of the BW maintenance fleet, continuing in service until the late 1990s. *Sagitta* was then transferred to be used as an educational centre. Staffordshire Environmental Trust assisted with the cost of converting the 1982 cabin into a representation of the 1930s living accommodation and the hull into a classroom.

Scorpio continued carrying as part of the post-nationalisation BW fleet and in the 1960s was transferred to the maintenance fleet and worked out of Norbury Maintenance Yard. Used as a piling boat in the 1970s, *Scorpio* retained her original riveted cabin until the early 1980s, when a new welded cabin was fitted at Teddersley Boat Yard in Goole. Her restoration has included fitting a new riveted cabin, shutt flooring, running gear and stand pump.

The Working Boats Project has made an important contribution to the preservation of some of the historic working boats that have managed to survive. A great deal of this work has been possible only because of lottery funding and it is important that future funding is secured to maintain those examples already saved and to take steps to protect others. **W**

All photos British Waterways, unless stated.

The ex-Gloucester & Sharpness New Docks Co canal tug of 1912 *Birmingham* now forms part of a permanent display at Tardebigge Maintenance Yard.
Simon V Hopkins

One of the few surviving cargo barges used for the traffic of coal, this joey boat at Bradley in 2001 was set for a happy future.

FRED DIBNAH
A MUCH LOVED STEEPLEJACK

A new and exciting book from the makers of the acclaimed film "Remembering Fred Dibnah"
This is the ultimate tribute to one of Great Britain's best loved television personalities.

A4 hard backed book

30 pages

Over 20 chapters

Includes free 70 minute CD released for the first time. Fred Dibnah live on stage

The Stories of a Steeplejack" worth £12.99.

Over 50 previously unreleased photographs, plus 30 high quality illustrations by international artist Brian Smith.

Includes articles written by Fred himself, Paul Donoghue, plus Fred's widow Sheila Dibnah, gives a true account of the last eight years of Fred's life. Chapters include:

Before he was famous.
They came from the BBC.
The Yard at Radcliffe Road.
Fred visits The Great Dorset Steam Fair
Fred and Steam Rallies.
So much to do? So little time?
The Final Journey.
The Legacy of a Legend.

Plus many more great stories

ISBN 1-59971-963-0

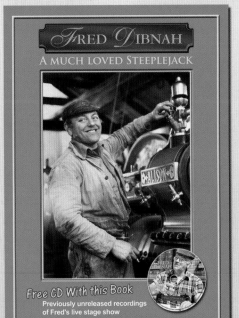

This new book from Rallyscene is the ultimate tribute to the late Fred Dibnah M.B.E. Researched over 16 years and shelved for the last 8 years of Fred's life, this book brings you closer to the real Fred Dibnah than you have ever been allowed before.

Fred co-operated with this book 100% in life, and it is a shame that the public has had to wait till after Fred's death to enjoy some of the stories that were written a long time ago.

Rallyscene are delighted that Sheila Dibnah (Fred's widow) has assisted in the production of this book. Sheila has made an astounding contribution by allowing the public full access to the last eight years of her life with the most famous Steeplejack in the world.

£19.95 Introductory Special Offer
plus £4.00 postage and packing

WITH FREE AUDIO CD

A perfect gift for any Fred Dibnah fan!

A £1 donation from the sale of every book will be made to "The Fred Dibnah Memorial Fund" on all sales through the Rallyscene Call Centre.

CREDIT CARD HOTLINE
0870 7890569

AVAILABLE ONLINE AT
www.freddibnah.tv

NORMALLY POSTED WITHIN 14 DAYS

LINES OPEN 24 HOURS 7 DAYS A WEEK

excellence in production
Rallyscene Logo is a registered trade mark No 2386784

Please send cash, cheques and postal orders payable to RALLYSCENE, to:
RALLYSCENE The Pond House, 59 Rotherham Road, Clowne, Chesterfield, Derbyshire. S43 4PT   Email: rallyscene@aol.com

Fred Dibnah
and the
canal tunnel

By Roger Murray

Fred was stuck and the boat was moving.
"Hang on, cock! I'll be down in a minute,"
he shouted not really aware of the seriousness
of the maritime incident unfolding below.

Steeplejack, steam buff and TV star the late Fred Dibnah was always fascinated by canals. He used to say: "Just think back to those hard days when men sweated with just shovel and pick and some swanky lord coming along and saying to the Government, 'Oh, we'll just dig a ditch from here to London, fill it with water and float boats down it, and carry cargo'. And they did it! We can't even dig a bloody pond in the garden today without it leaking."

He always maintained the canals and navigable rivers were fundamental to the success of the Industrial Revolution as they would never have been able to move many of the heavy castings over the roads which were just muddy quagmires, and they would certainly never have got them to the seaports for export.

His unwavering interests in things industrial and Victorian could have been nurtured at an early age by the disused Bolton and Bury Canal, just a few minutes from where Fred used to live with his mum and dad. It provided a colourful *Treasure Island,* full of hidden booty, a boyhood River Amazon to explore.

With his best mate, Alan Heap, he recovered all kinds of bygone industrial objects from the canal and the much-coveted treasure was stored in Fred's back yard. They even designed a crude diver's helmet to allow Fred to explore further into the murky uncharted depths.

Fred was a real owt-for-nowt merchant, as he would proudly proclaim. It was possibly those early canal forays which got Fred into the hoarding habit. He developed a keen nose for sniffing out discarded bits and pieces of Victorian engineering, which would be handy for the whimsical workshop he was building in his Bolton back garden, steam-driven, of course, by the beloved Aveling & Porter steamroller *Betsy.*

It all started with the erection of a simple shed supported by four telegraph poles just to house the steamroller. Then it seemed to sprout out all over the place with more telegraph poles and sheds housing medieval bits of machinery, all run by *Betsy's* flywheel, which was set up to drive an assembly of creaking, overhead line shafting. It really was like *Willie Wonka's Chocolate Factory.* When in full motion, everything shook!

The chuffing of the engine, the clattering of the machinery and the whirring of the line shafting pulleys within this conglomerate of shaking sheds created a rich backcloth to behold, especially with Fred running around in the midst of it, clutching tongs while brandishing a red hot bar of metal which was

Below: Fred always enjoyed his visits to canal installations and none more so than his trip in 2004 to the Anderton Boat Lift. Lynn Pegler, communications manager British Waterways (Wales and Border Counties) was his guide on that occasion and they are pictured together at the top of the lift. Author

being battered. Sparks flew as he shaped it under a prehistoric-looking mechanical hammer, the likes of which might never be seen again. It was something which could only have been built by dear Fred!

Fred's collection evolved slowly over the years. In nearly every factory or mill where he carried out work, he would ferret out some rusty, unwanted relic that the owner would gladly give him to be added to this wondrous 'workshop of the north'.

During one particular mill visit he had his eye on some very old line shafting with a unique pulley arrangement, which the owner of a derelict mill said he could have – but he would have to get it out. It was next to a canal and the only way was through some doors on the canal side of the building. The mill was on the opposite side to the towpath, so its walls went straight down into the water. It was a boat job.

I had an old, ex-working narrowboat which Fred had been on a few times, so we had a mission. We put a couple of his red ladders on the cabin roof and off we went. It was so long ago that I cannot remember where the mill was, or whether it was before or after getting the line shafting, but I do recall that during the course of the journey we went through a long, dark tunnel.

We were chugging through this tunnel – and Fred was always very interested in the tunnels – when he suddenly shouted: "Stop, stop, whoa, go back, go back!"

We had just gone under an airshaft and he wanted to see how the tons of bricks were supported at the base. "Go back, go back!" he hollered, clambering on the cabin roof with his big boots.

I backed the boat up and within minutes he had a ladder up into the base of the airshaft. All I could see were his boots sticking out from the black hole in the tunnel roof. "Have you got a torch?" he yelled down. "Can you let me have that lump hammer?"

His gravelly voice coming out of the hole seemed to amplify as if coming out of a trombone, the echo rumbling along the tunnel for what seemed ages. Luckily, it was late in the season and there were no other boats about, or anybody from British Waterways.

Within minutes, it sounded as if there was a complete demolition job going on up the airshaft with loads of sludge and muck and bricks tumbling down on the cabin roof.

"What the **** are you doing, Fred?" I shouted up. "You could have the whole bloody roof collapsing! Come down. You're not supposed to be up there!" I had thoughts of the whole lot collapsing, with us and the boat never to be seen again! Canal tunnels are wet, dark, dank places – with thoughts of the

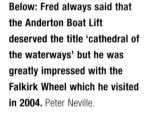

Below: Fred always said that the Anderton Boat Lift deserved the title 'cathedral of the waterways' but he was greatly impressed with the Falkirk Wheel which he visited in 2004. Peter Neville.

Fred, enjoying a cruise on the Weaver Navigation. Author.

Above: Fred is seen with BW engineer Tim Brownrigg. He is explaining that they need to swap seats as otherwise Tim is going to be talking to his duff ear! Author

the Kings, prodding in a screwdriver and gouging out a load of old cement and gunge, again falling on my head. I tried to look equally inspired. Evidently, according to Fred, they had used different types of bricks and cements in layers to counteract something which can happen in tunnels or air vents, which he seemed to know a lot about. He was totally absorbed and completely oblivious to the fact that we were on a boat, halfway through a tunnel, with a ladder stuck up a hole!

I was not paying attention, either, but the boat was gently moving forwards with the slow current of water and all of a sudden the ladder slipped on the wet, muddy, cabin roof and slithered sideways over the cabin side, taking me with it. I gave a yell and went down between the cabin side and the tunnel wall with my leg stuck through a rung. Being completely covered in slimy gunge I couldn't find a handhold. I yelled up to Fred that I was stuck and the boat was moving.

"Hang on, cock! I'll be down in a minute," he shouted, not really aware of the seriousness of the maritime incident unfolding below.

He was still happily banging away with loads of muck coming down clattering all over the cabin top. With the boat slowly moving forward, the airshaft hole was now nearly over the stern. I had visions of the boat drifting off leaving me in the water and Fred up the hole. I managed to grab the tiller and lever myself up. The ladder had demolished the stove chimney and wiped my bike off the roof, which was dangling in the water on the other side of the cabin.

Completely unfazed by the situation, Fred shouted down: "Are you going to make a pot of tea, Rog?" This was followed by a big thud as he jumped down. His boot marks were imprinted on the cabin roof of that boat until the day I sold it. They could probably add to its value now! We finally emerged from the tunnel with the boat looking as if it had just been salvaged from the bottom of the Mersey.

Fred was totally focused on the way that tunnel was built back in Victorian times. He was intrigued with the airshafts and how they managed to support the great weight of bricks, which, he reckoned, would be many tons as they went all the way up to the surface. As he said, it was the same principle as a mill chimney, but a mill chimney had solid ground to support it. I think he said they were built downwards instead of upwards, like a pit shaft, or something like that! I was more interested in getting away from the scene, especially as the British Waterways people could have heard the row emitting from the tunnel on that peaceful autumn afternoon. **W**

creature Gollum *(Lord of the Rings)* – and this was no exception. I just wanted to get him down and for us to get out of the place but he was having none of it, scrabbling further up and sending even more debris down.

"Bob your head up, Rog, and have a look," he shouted. I gingerly climbed a few rungs of the ladder so my head was just in the opening. I was very wary of Fred's 'come up and have a look' invitations, as he once had me up a mill chimney, which was the worst thing I had ever done in my life. He shone the torch on some bricks dripping with slime and water, which was sloshing on my head and down my neck.

"They were bloody clever men in those days – just look at that!" he exclaimed as if he had just broken the seal of a tomb in the Valley of

UK canal tunnels
more than 1000 yards long

Tunnel	Canal	Length in yards
*Standedge	Huddersfield Narrow Canal	5698
*Dudley	Dudley Canal No 1 Line	3154
Blisworth	Grand Union Main Line	3057
Netherton	Netherton Tunnel Branch Canal	3027
Harecastle	Trent & Mersey Canal	2926
Kings Norton	Worcester & Birmingham Canal	2726
Braunston	Grand Union Main Line	2048
Foulridge	Leeds & Liverpool Canal	1640
Crick	Grand Union (Leicester section)	1528
Preston Brook	Trent & Mersey Canal	1239
Husbands Bosworth	Grand Union (Leicester section)	1166

*Standedge and *Dudley tunnels can not be navigated by boats with internal combustion (or steam) engines under their own power. In the case of Standedge, boats are generally towed through in convoy style by a British Waterways-owned electrically powered tug.
The depths of Dudley tunnel can, on the other hand, be enjoyed by taking a voyage on a trip boat. The Dudley Canals Trust runs boats through the full length of the tunnel and to the connecting limestone mines. It also operates a journey on the open canal from Factory Junction to Merry Hill Waterfront and round trips involving the mines plus Dudley and Netherton Tunnels. Throughout the year it also holds many special events involving Dudley Tunnel including Jazz in the Mines, Ghost Tours and Santa Specials. More information at www.dudleytunneltrips.org

Heading down to the Cheshire plain! The narrow boat *Hunky Dory* is seen leaving Audlem Lock 13 on the Shropshire Union Canal. Author.

Meet the Association of Waterways Cruising Clubs

While mooring at an attractive, remote spot on any waterway is one of the pleasures of cruising, breaking down miles from anywhere can be a daunting prospect.

Forty years ago the late Dennis Cole, then commodore of St Pancras Cruising Club, faced this problem when his outboard engine packed up at Marsworth while on a cruise from St Pancras Cruising Club along the Grand Union Canal. Boatyards were few and far between in those days but Dennis knew about the existence of the Dunstable and District Boat Club at Cook's Wharf, Pitstone, nearby. He called the club's commodore, who alerted an engineer and, as a result, Dennis was soon under way again.

The recovery prompted him to arrange a meeting between St Pancras, Dunstable, Uxbridge and Lee & Stort boat clubs to discuss a scheme for a formal inter-club arrangement to provide an emergency service for boaters. As a direct result of that meeting the Association of Waterways Cruising Clubs (AWCC) was formed in 1964. Its function was not only to give practical help to boaters of member clubs but also to offer safe overnight moorings provided, of course, that a berth was available.

Its growth was rapid: by 1966 membership had increased from four to 18 clubs flying the AWCC's blue and yellow burgee, and the first handbook was published giving club locations and

Above: St Pancras Cruising Club boats in the heart of London. Malcolm Wood.

emergency telephone numbers. A summer dance was held aboard one of the Thames river boats and the first rally was held at Gayton Junction on the Grand Union. In the mid-70s, when the number of clubs passed the half-century mark, it was decided to reform the association, applying the regional structure that remains to this day.

By 1979 the number of participating clubs had risen to 80 members and AWCC had become a recognised and respected consulting authority on boating affairs. Although the membership curve then flattened out, in part owing to the demise of some clubs and the amalgamation of others, in general the AWCC continued to take more clubs on board. The Association of Waterways Cruising Clubs now has more than 100 associate clubs representing some 20,000 members covering the whole of the inland waterways network from Lancaster to London, Boston to Bristol and Ripon to Reading.

The AWCC has also grown in stature. In addition to providing breakdown assistance and temporary moorings, it has become an influential boaters' lobby, consulted by British Waterways, the Environment Agency and independent navigation authorities as well as IWAAC, district and local councils and the DETR. The association also works closely with navigation user groups including the Inland Waterways Association, Royal Yachting Association, National Association of Boat Owners, British Marine Industry Federation and the Association of Pleasure Craft Operators.

Mindful that local issues concern boaters as much as national developments, the AWCC lends its support to individual clubs through six regional committees covering London, the Midlands, north-east, north-west, south-east and south-west. Each member club has a vote at national level and is represented on the local

Top: The association's Midland region rally in 2002 at Longwood Boat Club. Malcolm Wood.

Above: St Pancras Cruising Club boats at Limehouse waiting to cruise the tidal Thames. Malcolm Wood.

area committee. Apart from regular meetings, the AWCC distributes its newsletter *Alert*, reporting on news, expressing views and explaining actions taken. *Alert* is also accessible on the AWCC's own web page. An annual handbook lists all member clubs, giving locations, club contacts and the facilities available in case of need.

The association has always supported comprehensive insurance for boats and offers its own scheme through one of the major underwriters. AWCC also offers professional advice on safety matters with its own Risk Assessment CD available to all clubs and there is also financial and taxation advice available.

Now that more boaters are able to enjoy extended cruising and are 'weekending' their boats around the waterways network, members of affiliated clubs have an immediate entry to clubs en route. Clubs with premises welcome

visiting boaters to use their facilities, have a drink at the bar and, like all boaters do, swap stories about their adventures afloat. Thanks to the unique facility, a number of new and long lasting friendships are being made all around the system.

Why not take a look at the AWCC web pages where you can find a contact for every club around the system on the 'club finder' page: www.awcc.org.uk **W**

If you want further details of what AWC has to offer, contact the National Secretary
Keith Noble
69 Downs Drive
West Timperley
Altrincham
Cheshire WA14 5QT.
Tel 0161 9693776
Email keithnoble_awcc@yahoo.co.uk

Top: St Pancras Cruising Club bar in the process of being built by members. Denise Keir.

Above: The dry dock under construction by members at St Pancras Cruising Club. Denise Keir.

The amazing Falkirk Wheel

This specially commissioned aerial picture was taken using a kite. James Gentles (c). www.gentles.info/KAP

The Falkirk Wheel is the spectacular centrepiece of the Millennium Link. The structure cost a reported £17-million to build while the complete link was in the region of £80-million. Developed by British Waterways, the 'wheel' is their biggest engineering project undertaken in Scotland.

The Millennium Link reconnects the Union Canal with the Forth & Clyde Canal and re-establishes east to west coast access for boats. The Forth & Clyde Canal was the world's first man-made, sea-to-sea ship canal, and re'connecting it to the Union Canal at Falkirk restored the waterway link between the cities of Edinburgh and Glasgow.

Work to relink the two canals, which are 115ft (25 metres) apart, started in 1999 and the spectacular project was opened by the Queen on Friday 24 May 2002.

The Union Canal was opened in 1822 and it is one of two lowland canals in Scotland. As built, the Union was 31½ miles (50.6km) long and it was often referred to as 'a mathematical river', it being built on a natural 240ft (73m) contour line, thus eliminating the need for locks. As well as providing a waterways link between Glasgow and Edinburgh, by way of a connection with the Forth & Clyde Canal at Falkirk, the canal was intended as a coal-carrying route between Scotland's coalfields and Edinburgh. The name

'Union' reflected the act of linking the two cities. The by-then-underused canal closed to traffic in 1965.

The idea of building a canal across central Scotland was proposed during the reign of Charles II but work was not started on the cut, to be called the Forth & Clyde Canal, until the middle of the 18th century. The canal is 35 miles (56.3km) long and runs from Bowling on the River Clyde to Grangemouth on the River Forth. It was the first canal to be completed in Scotland and was undoubtedly a major engineering feat, having some 39 locks. The canal closed on 1 January 1963 and in its restored condition was reopened by Prince of Wales in 2001.

Many barriers had to be overcome during the construction of the Millenium Link thanks to other building and motorway work filled in the cut and removed locks. For example, a new stretch of canal had to be dug at Wester Hailes and, where it was cut by the M8, the Union Canal was diverted a little to the west through an entirely new channel. Most significantly, a way had to be found of linking the canals together in the absence of the 11 locks that used to do that job. The answer was an extension to the Union Canal leading to the top of the magnificent Falkirk Wheel. **W**

Courtesy British Waterways.

All pictures Peter Neville © Toadstone.com.

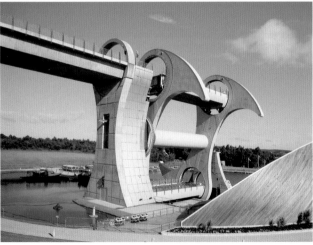

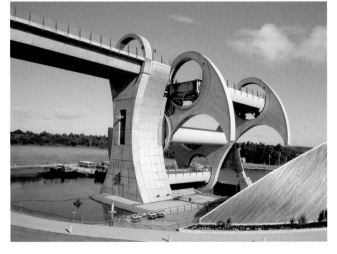

Falkirk Wheel Fact File

- First structure of its kind in the world.
- Design life of at least 120 years.
- 35m high x 35m wide x 30m long.
- Each gondola contains at least 250,000 litres of water.
- Capable of carrying eight boats at a time.
- A single trip will take 15 minutes.
- Opened as part of the Millennium Link on 24 May 2002.

The Falkirk Wheel is the world's first rotating boat lift. The 35m high, 1500 tonne machine transports canal barges and other boats between the Forth & Clyde and the Union Canals, a vertical drop of 18 metres. Before the closure of the canals in the mid-20th century, this transfer was achieved by a flight of 11 locks.

The wheel has an outside diameter of 35m, and comprises two 1.4m wide steel clawed arms rotating on a 3.5m diameter axle. A pair of 25m long, 300m3 water-filled caissons (or 'gondolas') act as containers for boats that are lifted through the 24m vertical distance between the two canals. Drive is provided at one end of the axle through a system of hydraulic planetary gear units, with stability of the caissons ensured by a network of synchronised gears. It is capable of carrying a total payload of 600 tonnes in winds of Force 6 (25-31mph).

Bachy/Soletanche and Morrison Construction Joint Venture won the contract to design and construct a new section of canal, a tunnel beneath the Antonine wall, a section of aqueduct, the wheel and receiving basin. In turn the Joint Venture appointed Butterley Engineering to design and construct the wheel. Butterley undertook all construction work for the wheel and set up its own team to carry out the design work. This team comprised Tony Gee and Partners, to undertake the structural design responsibilities and MG Bennett & Associates to design the mechanical and electrical equipment for the wheel.

The wheel's manufacturers have a real waterways heritage connection. The Derbyshire-based Butterley Engineering Co was founded in 1790 by canal engineers Benjamin Outram and William Jessop. In the past the firm has built many lifting and fixed bridges across waterways. The pieces of the wheel were all first welded at Butterley and afterwards erected on site using 15,000 nuts and bolts. The complete structure weighs 1300 tonnes plus 500 tonnes of water. The pieces were transported to the site by road, in lorry-size loads from the firm's works. **W**
Technical specification courtesy of British Waterways.

Meet AINA

The Association of Inland Navigation Authorities (AINA) is the industry body in the UK for inland navigation authorities. AINA was set up in December 1996 with strong encouragement from the Government to provide, for the first time, a single voice on waterway management issues. The broad purpose of AINA is to facilitate the management, maintenance and development of the inland waterways as an economic, environmental, recreational and social resource.

AINA currently has 28 members. They include local authorities, national park authorities, drainage commissioners, port and harbour authorities, original canal companies, the National Trust and other charitable trusts, in addition to the three large publicly funded navigation authorities – British Waterways, the Environment Agency and the Broads Authority. Between them, AINA members own, operate and manage some 5000km of waterway, which represent almost a complete coverage of Britain's inland waterways.

While each member of AINA has its own constitution, aims and objectives and, in many cases, Acts of Parliament regulating the operation of its waterways, the resource capabilities available to members in financial and human terms vary enormously; a number of members operate almost exclusively through volunteer effort.

The Wey & Arun Canal Trust is an associate members of AINA. The delightful scene at Brewhurst Bridge was captured on a glorious February day in 2002. Alan Barnes.

Full members
Basingstoke Canal Authority
Bristol Harbour Authority
British Waterways
Broads Authority
Cardiff Harbour Authority
Chelmer & Blackwater Navigation Ltd (Essex Waterways)
Conservators of the River Cam
Devon County Council
Driffield Navigation Ltd
Environment Agency
Exeter City Council
Lower Avon Navigation Trust Ltd
Lake District National Park Authority
Loch Lomond & The Trossachs NPA
Manchester Ship Canal Company
Middle Level Commissioners
Company of Proprietors of the Neath Canal Navigation
Port of London Authority
Upper Avon Navigation Trust
The Wey Navigations (National Trust)

Associate members
Bude Canal Trust
Droitwich Canals Trust Ltd
Herefordshire & Gloucestershire Canal Trust
Sleaford Navigation Trust
Company of Proprietors of the Stroudwater Navigation
The Wey & Arun Canal Trust

Affiliate members
Neath Port Talbot County Borough Council
The Waterways Trust

AINA can be contacted at Fearns Wharf, Neptune Street, Leeds LS9 8PB
Tel 0113 2433125
Fax 0113 2458394
Website www.aina.org.uk

Association of Inland Navigation Authorities

WOODWORKS BOAT FITTING
Est. 1997

High Quality Custom Boats

www.boat-fitting.co.uk

Unit 72, Road B, Boughton Ind. Est. New Ollerton, Notts. NG22 9LD

01623 860 553

email: info@boat-fitting.co.uk

Proprietor: *Andrew C. Hooke B.A. (Hons)*

British Marine Federation

SHOBNALL MARINA

With everything for the boat owner

◆ Covered dry dock (DIY or serviced)
 • paint dock • extensivly stocked chandlery
 • signwriting/painting • gas/diesel/pumpout
 • mechanical & joinery work • call-out service
 • CORGI gas fitter • Marine surveyor &
 BSS examiner • Boats always for sale

◆ *On-line chandlery – www.jannel.co.uk*

JANNEL CRUISERS

SHOBNALL MARINA, SHOBNALL ROAD,
BURTON UPON TRENT, STAFFS DE14 2AU
TEL: 01283 542718 FAX: 01283 545369
email: boats@jannel.co.uk web: www.jannel.co.uk

BLUE WATER MARINA LTD

The largest selection of new and used narrowboats in the North of England

Open 7 Days A Week

• New Shells • Sailaways
• Fully Fitted boats • Wide Beams

• Brokerage • Outright Purchase • Part Exchange

Please visit our website for detailed information including external and internal photographs of all boats for sale

www.bluewatermarina.co.uk

South End, Thorne, South Yorkshire DN8 5QR
Tel/Fax: 01405 813165
mail@bluewatermarina.co.uk

 # T.R Boat Handling

RYA Recognised Teaching Establishment

"I would have no hesitation in recommending your course to any other disabled person"
John - Birmingham

THE IDEAL PRESENT THAT LASTS FOREVER

• 1, 2 and 3 days RYA courses aboard our own narrowboat or your own craft.

• RYA Inland Waterway Helmsman certificate for both beginners and the experienced from £90.00.

• Friendly and understanding instructor, also ICC & CEVNI courses MCA boat master grade 3.

"Your pleasant teaching skills soon had Sue relaxed and her confidence was obvious by the end of the day".
Ray & Sue - Nottingham

BOOK YOUR COURSE NOW

Tel: 01785 824012 Mob: 07947 337492

71

The way it was

Classic millscapes: 'The Weavers Triangle' on the Leeds – Liverpool Canal, Burnley, Lancashire. Alan McEwen Collection.

Classic millscapes: Aston-under-Lyne Canal, near Ancoats in Greater Manchester. Alan McEwen Collection.

Wharf House Narrowboats

Boat Builders and Chandlers

Winners of 'Favourite Boat' at Crick Show 2003 & 2005

The **Chandlery** stocks a wide range of products which we are constantly expanding, and as boat builders ourselves, we particularly specialise in help and advice for those fitting out their own boats.

Specialising in Advanced Electrical Systems for boats

WH285613H

For more details ring
Phill or Sue Abbott on 01788 899041
or Fax 01788 891535
or come and see us at Bottom Lock,
Dark Lane, Braunston, Northants NN11 7HJ

phillabbott@wharfhouse.co.uk

Visit our website: www.wharfhouse.co.uk

RELAX,
you've chosen Blakes

WORLD-CLASS PAINTS

Swanwick Marina, Lower Swanwick, Southampton, Hampshire SO31 7EF
T: 01489 864440 F: 01489 564011 E: blakes_sales@uk.hempel.com www.blakespaints.com

BLAKES
Paints

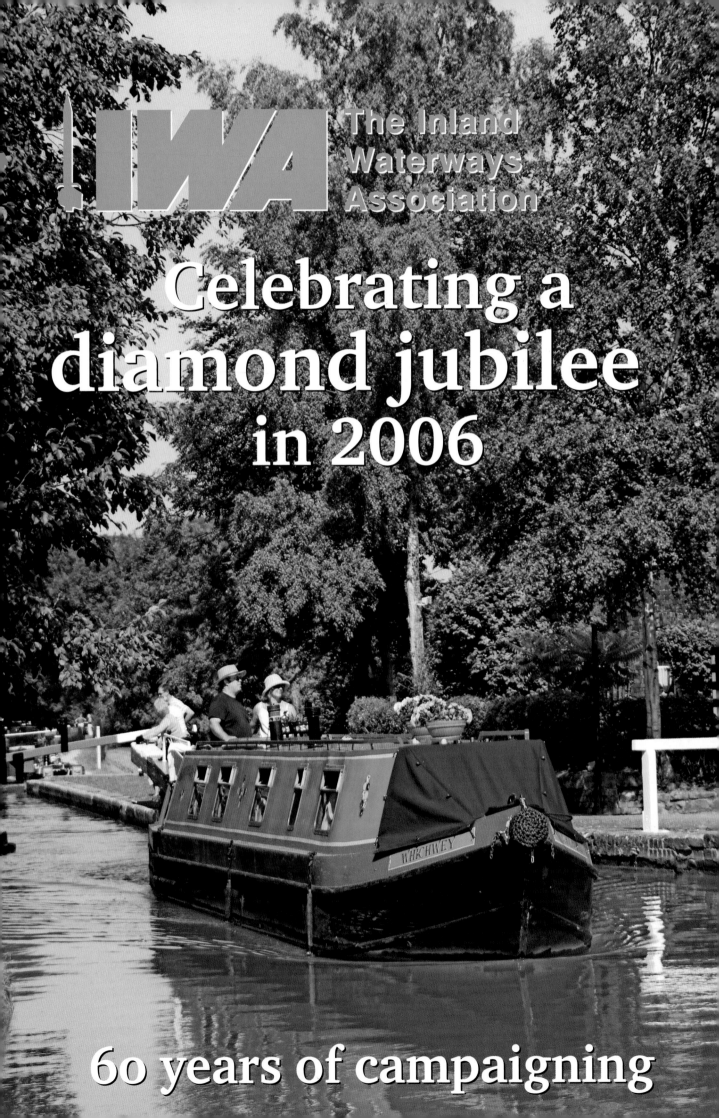

The Inland Waterways Association

Celebrating a diamond jubilee in 2006

60 years of campaigning

Inland Waterways Association campaigning for 60 years! 2006 is IWA's diamond jubilee year and the organisation is still tirelessly working to protect our waterways heritage.

Every year more than 10-million people visit Britain's waterways to cruise, canoe, fish, walk the towpath, observe wildlife – and enjoy the sheer splendour of the engineering and scenic surroundings of our canals and navigable rivers. It may seem hard to believe that, just a few decades ago, these exceptional places of peace and relaxation were very nearly lost to us forever.

In the 80 years or so up to 1850, a generation of engineering visionaries designed and built more than 4000 miles of canals. Together with improvements to river navigations, the canal system created the first countrywide transport network capable of carrying vast quantities of freight. It provided the lifeblood without which the Industrial Revolution could not have taken place.

Many thousands of horse-drawn boats carried coal and raw materials to the new manufacturing centres and then distributed the manufactured goods. The countryside also benefited as farm produce was transported by water right to the very hub of Britain's major towns and cities. The 'canal mania' of the early 1800s was, however, brought swiftly to a halt by the coming of the railways. That started the steady decline of the national waterways network, which began to crumble and fall into disuse even before it was fully completed.

In 1944 the book *Narrow Boat* by LTC Rolt was published and touched a chord with a large section of the British public. It described the author's journey in 1939 around the canals in his narrowboat Cressy. The book captured the spirit of the fast-declining waterways and of the special breed of people who lived and worked on them.

One of the many people who wrote to Tom Rolt after reading *Narrow Boat* was the then literary agent and aspiring author, Robert Aickman. He was the one who gave Rolt the idea of forming a society to campaign for the regeneration of the canals. Accordingly, in 1946 The Inland Waterways Association was born.

Now, 60 years on, The Inland Waterways Association (IWA) remains committed to the conservation and restoration of Britain's network of canals and navigable rivers. Our inland waterways are probably used more widely now than at any other time in their history and this is testimony in part to what IWA has achieved so far.

Years of effort by the association, with its relentless campaigning aimed at changing policies and attitudes, prevented the Llangollen Canal, the southern Oxford and the Leeds & Liverpool, to name but a few, from being abandoned and forgotten forever. Massive fundraising and volunteer work parties helped to restore and reopen waterways like the southern Stratford-upon-Avon Canal and River Avon navigations in those early days.

Since the association was founded, more than 500 miles of canals and navigable rivers have been returned to public use – with a further 500 miles of derelict inland waterways

Above: An idyllic scene on the River Nene at Fotheringay Castle. Robin Jones.

Top: The IWA encourage boaters to get together at special events. Doug Small.

Above left: IWA events are not only a great day out for boaters but also provide fantastic entertainment for all the family. Waterway Images.

Above right: This was Preston Brook in 2005. The national festival and boat show takes place annually over the August Bank Holiday weekend. Waterway Images.

now the subject of future restoration plans. It demonstrates, therefore, what can be achieved with financial support and the efforts of a willing volunteer workforce, as personified by IWA branch members and their associated Waterway Recovery Group.

The Waterway Recovery Group (WRG) since its formation in 1970 has physically undertaken the restoration of derelict waterways and associated structures. It has played a major role in the restoration of Britain's canal network. In these modern times the WRG also acts as a national co-ordinating body for volunteer labour on our inland waterways and provides equipment, expertise and publicity for restoration projects. WRG runs 'canal camps' based on different restoration projects throughout the country and invites volunteers

to 'have a dirty weekend' and get involved in the active restoration of Britain's many and diverse waterways.

As an important part of a firm IWA commitment to the waterways system, the association awards numerous grants to restoration projects. For example, in 2005 IWA made a £15,000 contribution to the Cotswold Canals Trust. That award helped to fund the reconstruction of Pike Bridge on the Stroudwater Navigation in Gloucestershire. A further £10,000 given to the Grantham Canal Partnership was put towards the cost of a feasibility study to determine a route to reconnect that canal with the River Trent in Nottinghamshire. Over the last 30 years, IWA has donated to projects in excess of £2-million – a truly impressive sum of money.

Opportunities and threats remain ever-present so there is much still to be done. For instance, to secure the future of the Chelmer and Blackwater Navigation in Essex, IWA has taken over the management of the waterway, so preventing the navigation company going into liquidation. The association has also offered to provide financial, advisory and physical support to recreate the junction between the Wilts and Berks Canal and the River Thames in Oxfordshire, which they see as a fitting project for 2006, the year of the association's all diamond jubilee.

Waterways festivals

The IWA continues to encourage greater awareness of the waterways through its waterways festivals. The association has been staging them since 1950, and each year these events are held in a different part of the country in order to enable local waterways groups to bring 'their' projects to the attention of the many festival visitors.

IWA National Festival and Boat Show
The National Festival and Boat Show takes place annually over the August Bank Holiday weekend and is not only a great day out for boaters but also provides fantastic entertainment for all the family: Wild Over Waterways (WOW) activities for the children, an extensive selection of catering outlets, craft workshops and live music, all with the added bonus of free parking. Any profits made by the festival go back into funding the work of IWA.

The 2007 National Festival and Boat Show will take place at Hemingford Meadows, opposite St Ives on the picturesque River Great Ouse in Cambridgeshire. Many boaters on the Great Ouse and its tributaries will not previously have had the opportunity to participate in an IWA festival. It is also hoped that people from elsewhere in the country attending the festival will make the most of this unique opportunity to explore the Fenland waterway system.

Canalway Cavalcade

The Canalway Cavalcade takes place annually over the May Day Bank Holiday weekend in the picturesque setting of Little Venice – at the junction of the Regent's Canal and the Paddington Arm of the Grand Union Canal in London. There is a pageant of decorated boats, a procession of illuminated boats, a boat-handling competition, trade stalls, entertainments, real ale bar, puppet shows and WOW activities for children.

IWA national campaign rally
The national campaign rally is held annually over the Spring Bank Holiday weekend at the

Top left: The canals can be just as picturesque in winter! Ralph Freeman.

Top right: Britain's waterway network is a haven for wildlife. Author.

Above: The waterways are now popular locations for holidays and weekend breaks. Author.

Above: Pike Bridge on the Stroudwater Canal – a project that received funding from the IWA. Author.

end of May. The site for the campaign rally is chosen to raise awareness of a specific project or highlight the need for restoration of a particular canal.

The 2006 rally was held at Brookwood on the Basingstoke Canal in Surrey. The objective of the rally was to promote awareness of the need to safeguard and ensure the long-term future of the Basingstoke Canal as a navigable waterway and to celebrate the achievements of volunteers working on the canal's restoration. Boats gather from all over the waterway network for a weekend of entertainment, craft stalls, talks, Waterway Society stands and boaters' parades.

IWA national trailboat festival
The trailboat festival takes place over the Easter weekend. The venue changes yearly but, as with the national campaign rally, the site is chosen to raise awareness of a particular restoration project. Unlike the national campaign rally, the flexibility of trailboats means that a site can be chosen that is unconnected to the national waterway system.

Past trailboat festivals have drawn attention to areas previously unconnected to the waterways network. For example, in 1990 IWA took the unusual step of holding two trailboat festivals, one at Falkirk on the Forth & Clyde Canal in Scotland and the other at Hebden Bridge on the Rochdale Canal in West Yorkshire. After much campaigning, both canals have subsequently been fully restored and the Rochdale Canal is now reconnected to the national waterway network.

The 2006 national trailboat festival took place in April on the Northern Reaches of the Lancaster Canal in Cumbria and was not only a great opportunity for trailboaters to gather from all over the country but also offered visitors the opportunity to ride on a trip boat. A slipway was also constructed especially for the event offering trailboaters the opportunity to visit and still use the site long after the festival was over.

IWA narrow boat *Jubilee*

Narrow boat *Jubilee* is another way the association raises awareness of Britain's inland waterways. *Jubilee* serves as the floating information, publicity and campaigning vehicle for IWA. She was donated to the association in 1996, the year of IWA's golden jubilee – hence her name. Over the last 10 years, manned entirely by volunteers, she has travelled extensively throughout the canal and river network of England and Wales, extolling the benefits of conserving, restoring and developing inland waterways and their environment for everyone's benefit.

In the association's jubilee year the narrow boat of that name is undertaking a special Jubilee Journey. The planned journey is, in fact, a continuous voyage throughout the country before arriving at the IWA's National Festival and Boat Show at Beale Park, on the Thames, over the August Bank Holiday weekend. En route *Jubilee* has so far held a 'floating seminar', entertained civic dignitaries, council officials and television crews. Jubilee continues to help celebrate many important milestones in the association's 60-year history.

The future

The Inland Waterways Association will continue helping to bring life back to many more miles of long-derelict canals. In doing so it will also provide employment opportunities and help to develop wide-ranging leisure facilities. But politicians and planners have to be persuaded; the huge cost of restoration and future maintenance has to be secured. There are ever-present threats to the old canal routes from the conflicting needs for highway and building development.

Multi-million-pound grants from the Government, the national lottery and other sources have made a huge difference and many waterways restoration projects, including the Kennet & Avon, Rochdale and Huddersfield Narrow canals and the Anderton Boat Lift have benefited. In the first place, the funding bodies had to be persuaded – a process that involved many years of mounting hard-fought campaigns. Had it not been for the pump-priming grants, voluntary work parties and advice from IWA and local waterways societies, these high profile and truly spectacular projects would never have been successfully completed.

The IWA needs the support of everyone who cares about our waterways heritage to ensure its continued success. The lifeblood of the association is ultimately its members, whose invaluable help provides the funding and resources for a multiplicity of noteworthy campaigns. Most importantly, though, the larger the membership, the louder the voice! Thus the more notice people take of the Inland Waterways Association's views.

The backing of a large membership gives added weight to IWA's influence with politicians, both nationally and locally, with the mandarins in Whitehall, with navigation authorities and with all arms of the Government… in fact with everyone who makes decisions about our waterways.

Since 1946, IWA's membership has grown to more than 17,000. Become a member of The Inland Waterways Association, a force for good!

For information on how to join, call us on 01923 711 114 or visit www.waterways.org.uk/membership
Details of recovery group camps can be found at www.wrg.org.uk
More information on *Jubilee's* journey can be found at www.waterways.org.uk/nbjubilee
More information on IWA's festivals can be found at www.waterways.org.uk/festivals

Above: Waiting to be put back 'in water'. The canal bed between Pike Bridge and Dock Lock on the Stroudwater Canal. Author.

The Spectacular Douro Valley
by Steam Train and River Cruiser

Comfort and Friendship

At PTG Tours we pride ourselves on the enjoyment that you get from our unique holidays. On our special charter trains, whenever possible, first class carriages are used with a maximum of 30 people per coach giving everyone space to spread out. We only use quality hotels, normal 4 star. All our tours are limited to small groups leading to an unrivalled friendly atmosphere. Many of our customers have become good friends and return time and time again. PTG Tours Limited was established in 1998 and has built up a good strong reputation for quality and reliability

There is no better way to see these fascinating countries than travelling by train and staying at the finest hotels.

Plenty for Everyone

Our holidays are for anyone looking for something a bit different. They have a railway theme but include visits to historic cities, gardens, vineyards, port lodges, river cruises and much more. We use vintage locomotives (sometimes steam) and carriages, where available, therefore adding to the atmosphere. By using trains we allow you to see the most beautiful areas from the comfort of your First Class seat in the most relaxing and safest form of transport. Many of the areas we visit are only visible from the railway line.

Flexibility

We have regular tours throughout the year varying from one to ten days On most tours you have the option of joining the complete tour or just the days that interest you the most.

Douro Valley

Many of our tours include Portugal's most beautiful region, the port vineyards of the Douro Valley. This wide river valley was tamed by a series of dams in the 1970's enhancing the beauty of the area even more. The only way to se the area at its best is by train and river cruise. Our tours combine both forms of transport to give you an unforgetta experience. We also visit the spectacular Tamega, Corgo and Tua valleys which feed the Douro and are still served narrow gauge railways that cling to the sides of the mountains. Visits to vineyards, the palace of Mateus and port lodges complete the experience.

Portugal Spain and USA

We have a range of rail based holidays throughout the year to some of the most beautiful parts of the world including Galicia in Northern Spain, the luxury 'El Transcantabrico' rail-cruise along the north coast of Spain and trips to the USA including the Colorado Rockies.

Call us now and we will send you a copy of our free full colour brochure

PTG Tours Ltd, Gable House, Letcombe Hill, East Challow, Oxon, OX12 9RW
Tel/Fax: 01235 768855
Email: brunel@ptg.co.uk   Web: www.ptg.co.uk

WILLOW WREN
CRUISING HOLIDAYS

Rugby Wharf

Narrowboat hire and boatbuilding
On the North Oxford canal
Individual narrowboats built to a high standard
Hireboats from 2 to 12 berth
Including 30' Day Boat

For enquiries or to arrange a visit call

01788 562183

Or go to www.willowwren.co.uk

WI285507H

Fast becoming the
TALK OF THE TOWPATH

✦ **1,000's of items in stock**
✦ **Bargains galore**

Stock includes: Cookers - Hobs - Sinks - Fridges - Bath - Inverters - Chargers - VHF's - Toilets - Heaters and lots of Pumps

IF IT'S AVAILABLE - WE CAN SUPPLY IT

✦ Mooring & Yacht Services
✦ 20 Ton Travel Lift
✦ Maintenance, Repairs, Painting, etc.
✦ 2,000 sq. ft. Chandlery

PLASTIMO MarineMart LS
ecs JABSCO WAECO International
SHURflo STOVES Newhome
vetus ROADPRO Practical Products on the Move
Aquafax Aarrow Fires
THETFORD Albion
victron energy
STERLING International yachtpaint.com
NEW International Paints Major Stockist

VIKING MARINE

Tel/Fax: 01405 765737
Albert Street, Goole DN14 5SY

(On the Aire & Calder, first marina on right from Goole Port. By road, easy access between Doncaster & Hull, 2m from J36, M62)

VI285395H

www.vikingmarine.co.uk

Craftmaster paints

We have a considerable library of historic colours from all areas of heritage transport & are able to research or duplicate many more.

nit 3 Dadfords Bridge
nd Est,
lant Street,
Vordsley,
tourbridge DY8 5SY

el: 01384 485554

zita@craftmasterpaints.co.uk
ww.craftmasterpaints.co.uk

295550H

Basingstoke Canal
Surrey & Hampshire's Waterway

Discover 32 miles of nature reserve for walking, boating, fishing and cycling

The Canal Visitor Centre Mytchett is the perfect place to start exploring the Canal or simply relax and watch the boats pass by.

- Trail blazer play area
- Gift shop
- Tearoom
- Boat trips
- Picnic site
- Free parking

- Information point and helpful staff
- Camping
- Function room
- Easy access to 32 miles of Canal towpath

A great day out for all the family!

Pick up a free leaflet from your local information centre or contact us...

Tel 01252 370073
Canal Visitor Centre
Mytchett Place Road, Mytchett, GU16 6DD

info@basingstoke-canal.co.uk
www.basingstoke-canal.co.uk

Narrow boat *President*
and Fellows, Morton and Clayton

President, a unique steam-powered narrow boat, was built in 1909 at a cost of £600 by Fellows, Morton and Clayton at Saltley, Birmingham (formerly Thomas Clayton's yard). One of the directors of the company, Joshua Fellows, gave his name to the distinctively shaped 'Josher' hull, which has riveted wrought iron sides and a 3in elm bottom. The company built and operated 31 steamers between 1889 and 1931.

The specially developed compound steam engine and coke-fired boiler took up much valuable cargo space and, for that reason, the steamers were to be in service for a relatively short period of time. Steamers could carry only 18 tons, compared to more than 25 tons in a horse-drawn boat, but were powerful enough to tow several unpowered boats (butty boats). Steam narrow boats led directly to the speeding up of canal traffic that had previously in the main been powered by horses or sail. In their short but glorious career, the steamers showed the canal carriers that powered boats were the way forward and, in doing so, no doubt hastened the advent of the internal combustion engine.

Steamers usually worked 'fly', that is day and night, on the canals between London, Birmingham, Coventry, Derby, Leicester and Nottingham. President was converted from steam power in 1925. The craft was fitted with a Swedish-made Bolinder crude oil engine and she continued in work until being withdrawn in

1973, by her then owners British Waterways. The famous, faithfully restored narrow boat is now based, together with her 'butty boat' *Kildare*, at the Black Country Museum, where she is cared for and operated, in an authentic manner, by an association called the Friends of President.

Fellows, Morton and Clayton (FMC) was founded in 1837 by James Fellows. His son, Joshua, took over the company after his death and it is he who is credited with overseeing the successful growth of the firm. The Grand Junction Canal Company ceased trading in 1876 and, seeing an opportunity, Joshua, together with Price & Son, quickly formed the London and Staffordshire Carrying Company. Frederick Morton joined that company later in the same year and he supplied enough working capital to fund further expansion.

In 1887 the company, which had by that time changed its trading name to Fellows, Morton and Company, took over the business of the London and Midlands Carrying Company. In 1889 that company acquired the general carrying company of Thomas Clayton and so the famous firm of Fellows, Morton and Clayton was born. FMC acquired mainly horse-drawn craft during their takeover dealings but among the vessels to come under their ownership there were several steam-powered craft. They then built more 'steamers' at their own Saltley workshops and that work included the manufacture of their own design of marine steam engine.

The company were successful and gained a reputation for offering a fast service supported by efficient warehousing and daily distribution services. In the years after WWI they became the major suppliers of those all-important staple British comestibles, tea and sugar, to the majority of the retailers in the Birmingham area.

In addition they carried all types of groceries and perishables, even supplying Cadbury's with cocoa beans. Their craft also carried fair quantities of paper, metals, wood and cement.

In 1912 they experimented with internal combustion-powered craft and their prototype *Linda*, fitted with a Bolinder semi-diesel engine, was a huge success and set the pattern for many other designs. FMC did continue to thrive even when competing with the expanding railways throughout the 1920s and 30s; no doubt the door-to-door delivery service was their ace in the hole.

However, in 1948, without any prior warning, the company announced its first and, as it turned out only, trading loss. A panic among its stockholders resulted. That led to voluntary liquidation and, as they say, at the stroke of a pen, the firm was no more! When the canals were nationalised, all of FMC's assets were bought by the British Transport Commission. **W**

Information kindly supplied by the Black Country Living Museum and Friends of President. For more information contact http://www.nb-president.org.uk/ and http://www.bclm.co.uk
All *President* pictures Author.

Top left: The funnel folds down! *President* crewman Bob Crompton.

Top right: *Kildare* nearest the bank and *President* – note the two distinctive Josher bows.

Above left and right: The cramped living conditions aboard working boats are illustrated by this picture of a section of the cabin on *President*.

Opposite top: A period scene: *President* at the Black Country Museum canal basin berthed between Kildare and the former tar carrier *Stour*.

Opposite bottom: Another shot of *President* and *Kildare* at Whatcroft.

Above left: The current steam engine fitted in *President* is a Sissons single-cylinder 12/14hp unit but the Friends still hope one day to find an original FMC steam engine. This is a view of the engine looking aft.

Above right: The room taken up by the steam boiler can be seen.

Far right: The firebox.

Right: This is a view of the engine looking from the back cabin.

Background: *President* with the 'butty' *Kildare* in tow at Whatcroft on the Trent & Mersey Canal, 2005.

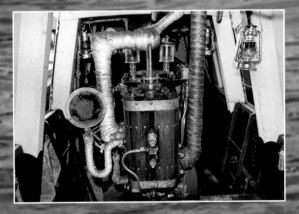

Cotswold canals
bringing the dream to life

This is the 'in water' pound between the restored Blunder lock (Stroudwater) and the as-yet-unrebuilt Pike lock. Facing west, away from Stroud.

T he mouth-watering prospect of reconnecting the rivers Thames and Severn by restoring the canal that bears the names of those rivers and the Stroudwater 'cut' has, of course, been talked about for many years. Recently an announcement of more funding for this ambitious project was made. The two 'cuts' are collectively referred to as the Cotswold Canals. Their return to water represents one of the new millennium's most exciting canal restoration schemes.

The Cotswold Canals comprise the 29-mile (46km) Thames & Severn Canal opened in 1789 and the seven-mile (13km) Stroudwater Navigation, which opened in 1779. If fully restored, the canals would form a continuous waterway from Saul Junction on the Gloucester and Sharpness Canal to Lechlade in Gloucestershire, including the two-and-a-half-mile (4km) Sapperton Tunnel and 56 locks.

The waterway at one time operated a passenger service between Gloucester and London. However, constant leakage problems on the canal and the advent of railway competition severely damaged its profitability. Around 1900 the canal was bought and improved by Gloucestershire County Council in an effort to stimulate canal traffic. Despite those efforts, the canal was abandonment as

unprofitable in 1933. Since then its line has been broken up and is now owned by more than 70 different landowners. The last trade boat reportedly worked on the Stroudwater in 1941, with that canal closing in 1954.

Originally the Stroudwater Canal section had its own junction with the River Severn and there is still physical evidence of that old waterways crossroad at Saul Junction on the Gloucester-Sharpness Canal. Any reconnected waterway from the Thames will terminate at Saul Junction and, accordingly, the Severn will actually be reached by way of the G&S.

At Saul Junction there is a length opposite the abandoned section which, up to Walk Bridge, is still in water and provides moorings for several craft next to Saul Boatyard and beyond British Waterways' Bridge House. After the 'in use' limit, the old canal continues by skirting attractively through the area of Whitminster before eventually meeting its first barrier on the way to a possible connection with the Thames.

That first blockage was caused some time ago by the upgrading of the A38 dual carriageway, and only a short distance farther on the as-built line of the Stroudwater Navigation is once again obstructed, this time by the formidable barrier of the M5. After the first two obstructions have been negotiated it is still not plain sailing to Stroud as there is the

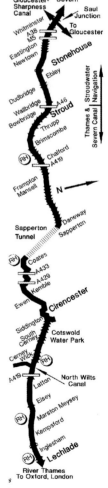

matter of the main Gloucester-Bristol railway line to take into consideration.

Reconnecting the complete Cotswold Canal system to the national waterway network is the stated and laudable aim of the partners in restoration. The lead partner in this huge undertaking is British Waterways, which is working with the Waterways Trust and the all-important Cotswold Canals Trust. The aim is an achievable one but the opening of a fully functioning through waterway connecting those two mighty rivers can only fairly be considered a long-term prospect.

The possible cost of the complete project has, not surprisingly, steadily increased since first its inception. In 2002 the quoted figure was £82-million, which included the cost of putting the historic Sapperton Tunnel back into use. That figure has now grown to £120-million but, say the partners, various costs have not been revisited since 2001, so the estimate takes into account only those original costs and inflation. The current figure is said to include the work to reopen the tunnel which British Waterways, following a 2001 feasibility study, estimated at £12-million.

The reopening of Sapperton Tunnel, say the Waterways Trust, does require further investigation. But they point out that it presents no greater challenge than did the

Top left: The new residential canalside development on the rebuilt Stroudwater at Ebley Mill is now well under way. Author.

Top right: The deep cutting that contains the Coates Portal of Sapperton Tunnel. What problems will be encountered when this historic structure is examined in detail? Author.

Right: *Perseverance* **is the watchword of the conservation movement and the Cotswold Canal Trust have thus aptly named their trip boat.** Sue Mills.

reopening of Standedge Tunnel on the Huddersfield, the longest, highest waterway tunnel, which was restored in 2002. Given the lapse in time since the last inspection, it would be fair to assume that the 2001 estimate for reopening Sapperton will rise considerably.

Sapperton Tunnel was first used more than 200 years ago and it was opened to traffic on 20 April 1789. The tunnel took five years to dig and, at 3817 yards (2·17 miles or 3·49km), it was at the time the longest tunnel dug in England. It still carries what remains of the Thames & Severn Canal under the highest part of the delightful Cotswold Hills and, at its deepest point, there is 70 yards (65m) of rock above the tunnel roof. It is now the third-longest canal tunnel in England.

The tunnel is almost in the centre of the Cotswold Canals and its reinstatement is crucial to the reopening of this historic cross-country waterway link. During its working life the section of canal containing the tunnel suffered badly from water loss through the region's particularly porous limestone.

Those operating difficulties were tolerated in the beginning as labour to repuddle was plentiful and cheap. The canal greatly reduced the cost of transporting coal from the Lancashire coalfields to Cirencester and also allowed a relatively speedy passage of boats between the west of England and London.

The tunnel's canal traffic started to tail off in the 1920s and a serious fall in the brick-lined section led to its closure in 1927. There are now thought to be several underground falls blocking the route. The tunnel area is a popular walking spot and there is road to a popular public house above the Coates Portal near Sapperton.

The recently announced Phase One funding of £11.9-million, squeezed from the constantly under-pressure HLF pot, will mean that a six-mile (9.65km) section of the former Stroudwater Navigation from Stonehouse to Brimscombe (via Stroud) can now be put back in place. Of course, that will simply be 'put in place' and not put 'completely in use' as far as most boaters are concerned because the completed waterway will, of course, be a landlocked section.

However, as the Waterways Trust are quick to point out, that short section will be welcomed by local residents inasmuch as it will provide an 'attractive linear water park' (their description). It will, they say, 'establish the principle of conservation-led restoration' and, in doing so, conserve 30 historic structures. In addition it will create a 16km multi-user trail extending to Saul, creating the

Below: Plaque at Brimscombe Port Trading Estate. Sue Mills.

Below: This is another view of Ebley showing the mill itself. Where the cut is shown blocked there will be a bridge when the building work is complete. Author.
Note: Both Ebley shots are rebuilt canal created by digging out a previous infill and both are Stroudwater Navigation. Both are downstream views looking east towards Stroud. Author.

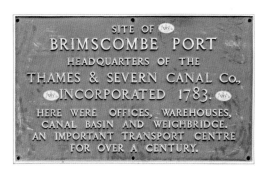

Top left: Blunder Lock (Stroudwater Navigation), which was restored in 1992. It was so called because a contractor purposely built its levels incorrectly following a grievance he had with the canal's bosses. Its original name was Lower Nassfield Lock. Author.

Top right: The overgrown canal bed of the Thames & Severn Canal as it passes through the picturesque area of Chalford Vale. The railway viaduct can be seen as it passes through the vale on the same line as the canal. Looking back towards Stroud to the west. Sue Mills.

Right: Looking in the direction of Stroud from the line of old River Severn connection of the Stroudwater Navigation, with the Gloucester & Sharpness Canal to the right and left and the 'in water arm' of the Stroudwater-to-Walk Bridge, which will be the restored canal's connection with the national network in the centre background. Author.

opportunity for people to become more active and to enjoy and understand the part the waterways played in the development of their community.

Some of the local residents, particularly those who owned property near the 'linear water park', were pleased with the new Phase One development in general and with the fact that they expected the value of their waterside properties to rise by at least 20 per cent in particular (if national patterns are repeated in Stroud).

As for the long-term protection of the natural habits of voles and crayfish, they were interested, if not ecstatic, when the benefits were pointed out. Experts say the current phase will create 600 full-time jobs and attract upwards of 215,000 extra visitors to the area. There is also a prediction of a £531,000 tourist spend to benefit the local economy.

However, there are local objections to the plan.

The areas either side of Sapperton Tunnel, including the villages of Chalford, Chalford Vale, Coates and Siddington, are very nice places to live in.

Will the reinstatement of this historically important waterway seriously affect quality of life? For the most part the waterway is well hidden from view and, as for noise, the pleasure craft won't be anything like as audible as the trains on the mainline which tunnel through Sapperton Hill next to the canal.

The objectors are genuinely concerned with the environmental issues, and rightly so! But then so are the scheme's partners and their professional advisers. Such projects are not embarked upon without feasibility and environmental impact studies being made.

Any reinstated canal would use the eight-mile-long pound between locks at its highest level (Daneway to Siddington) for water-holding, given the current obvious lack of a reservoir. To cope in busy times, however, the engineers all agree that a reasonable degree of back pumping will be required.

Cotswold Canal Trust chairman Bruce Hall and Waterways Trust chief executive Roger Hanbury explained why completing the section from Saul Junction (and thus linking into the national network) appears not to have been their first priority.

Both used the phrase 'it's the art of the possible'. By way of an explanation, they confirmed that the original intention was to restore from Stroud (Brimscombe Port) to Saul Junction (G&S) but that the funding was not available.

In January 2004 the partners submitted an unsuccessful application for £22.7-million from the HLF, which informed them that such a sum was not available at that time. Accordingly, they were asked to resubmit the application for approximately 50 per cent of that figure. They did so and have now received the £11.9-million to complete Phase One.

The Stonehouse to Brimscombe section could be deduced from their answers to have picked itself, given the overall cost, the cash available with matched funding from other sources and the requirements of the planners. The developers, Persimmon Homes, are busily pouring a great deal of their money into the impressive residential (and possibly commercial) canalside development at Ebley Mill, near Stroud.

To keep faith with the boaters and push their project further in the direction many see as the right one, the connection to Saul is now to be included in Phase Two. An application was submitted to the Big Lottery Fund for the £15.95-million needed in January 2006. No doubt that application will be examined during the summer of 2006 and hopefully the Cotswold Canal Trust will have something positive to report thereafter.

So what does this mean in practical, restored waterway terms?

- Brimscombe to Stonehouse (six-mile waterway) plus a walking trail to Saul: completion date 2008.
- Navigation Stonehouse to Saul (subject to Big Lottery application): completion date August 2010.
- Thames-to-Severn connection including reopening Sapperton Tunnel to boat traffic (via Gloucester & Sharpness Canal): no predicted date given.

Given the sheer size of the project, 2020 would not be an unreasonable target date; alternatively, given the availability of funding, it could, of course, happen a lot quicker than that! But then there is the small matter of a certain event being held in London in 2012! It would be nice to see the Olympic flame carried on a London-Stroud leg aboard a narrow boat. Perchance to dream!

In the meantime, buy a bottle of Champagne to celebrate the reopening; you can buy reasonably priced non-vintage now, and it should have aged nicely by then!

At the end of May 2006 the Cotswold Canals Trust were told their application for funding to help with Stonehouse-to-Saul part of the project had made the long list of 70 applications by Living Landmarks (part of the Big Lottery Fund) out of 700 applications. As a consequence, inspectors from the Big Lottery will be visiting the site and meeting the developing partners. The CCT will then be told before the end of the summer of 2006 whether their £25-million application has made the final shortlist.

Above: Boats of the Willows Trust (a registered charity) regularly ply the Gloucester & Sharpness Canal. Both of their boats are built to take up to 30 people with severe disabilities. They are both fully wheelchair accessible, and facilities include hydraulic lifts, toilets, large windows, central heating and full safety equipment. The *Leonard Matcham* is seen at Saul Junction. Sue Mills.

The canal at Stonehouse on the outskirts of Stroud. In this picture you could actually believe it is in use! Author.

Bronte Boats
CANAL CRUISING

LUXURY HOLIDAY HIRE BOATS AND CANAL CRUISES IN YORKSHIRE

SOUTH PENNINE RING
cruise the highest canal in the UK!

Explore Yorkshire's unspoilt waterways on one of our boats available for short breaks or weekly hire.
2 to 4/5 berth or 2 to 7 berth, all year round.
Fully equipped to ensure you have a wonderful relaxing holiday
Steering and lock tuition provided • Pets welcome

We also have an elegant Canal Cruise Boat providing one hour cruises, evening meal and lunchtime meal cruises, bar, wc, central heating.
Available for private hire for that special occasion!

Call for a brochure or see our website for full details.

Bronte Boats, The Marina, Hebden Bridge HX7 8AD West Yorkshire. 01422 845557. www.bronteboats.co.uk

ISA
Training Centre

- State of the art 21 foot yachts with canting keels
- Courses available for all levels of experience
- ½ day sessions to week long courses
- Yacht hire available

HODSON BAY SAILING

Phone +353 (0) 49 9529750
Email: info@hodsonbaysailing.com
Website: www.hodsonbaysailing.com

MILLAR MARINE
Chandlery

The Wharf at Shardlow, Trent and Mersey Canal

NOW IN OUR NEW PREMISES
(Formerly Shardlow Antiques)

- MORE SPACE
- MORE STOCK
- SAME QUALITY SERVICE

Parts & Accessories also available for Motorhomes, Caravans, Horse Boxes

web: www.millarmarine.com

Call Norman or Christine on 01332 793358

Warehouse C • 24 The Wharf • Shardlow • Derby • DE72 2GH • Fax: 01332 799167 • E-mail: sales@millarmarine.com

TOWPATH

TOWPATH TALK
The UK's No 1 newspaper for all waterway users

See Page 7 for exciting mooring development news....

RISING FEARS
Low river levels give cause for concern

In this issue...

SCADA 6
BW's state of the art water management system

Shannon Navigation 34
Lough Derg

Loughborough 38
Festival review

WIN a year's Bronze membership to River Canal Rescue's breakdown and recovery service – see page 38

Issue 4   11 May 2006   £1.65

TOWPATH TRADER
DESTINATION X - AYLESBURY
ALTERNATIVE FUEL SOLUTIONS

The UK canal network not only provides hours of pleasure for boaters, as in this typical scene at Pontcysyllte, but also a vital network for supplying that vital resource – water. Sue Mills

LUXURY CANAL-SIDE 4/5 BEDROOM HOUSE
1/5th acre, with mooring rights, in private Boat Basin off Grand Union Canal

Newport-Pagnell/Milton Keynes Area
Guide Price £465,000
Internet: **www.canal-house.us**

NOTTINGHAM *Castle* marina
NARROWBOATS WANTED
FOR BROKERAGE OR CASH SALE
SEE OUR MAIN ADVERT ON PAGE 23
Tel: 0845 270 5613
E-mail: Sales@notts-marina.co.uk

FIRST WITH THE NEWS EVERY THREE WE

Welcome to **Towpath Talk**! Towpath Talk is the only specialis
newspaper covering Britain's Waterways.

Towpath Talk is the way for you to keep in touch with the boatin
community and includes:

- Inland Waterways Holidays • Boating on the inland waterway
of the UK • Product Reviews • Boats For Sale and For Hire
- Food and Drink - Pubs and Restaurants along the canals
- Property For Sale • Brokerage
- Services, Parts, Spares and Equipment
- Insurance • Situations Vacant
- Plus we are the only
waterways publication
that can be read
completely online!

CALL **01507 529300** www.**towpathtalk**.cc
FOR FURTHER INFORMATION & SUBSCRIPTION DETA
Towpath Talk Mortons Media Group, Media Centre, Morton Way, Horncastle, Lincolnshire LN9

offer you an open invitation to visit their
magical
waterways

The Barrow Navigation
The Erne System
The Grand Canal
The Lower Bann
The Royal Canal
The Shannon-Erne Waterway
The Shannon Navigation

www.waterwaysireland.org

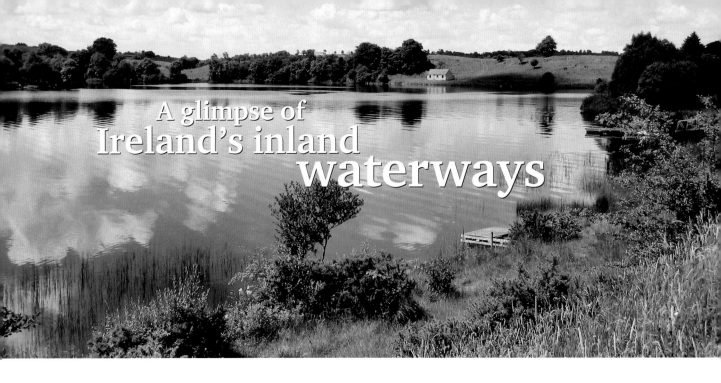

A glimpse of
Ireland's inland
waterways

Situated in a land of tranquil beauty shaped by legend and tradition, Ireland's waterways provide a unique experience for everyone. The country's natural environment provides excellent opportunities to participate in a huge range of sightseeing, cultural and outdoor activities. Be it adventure or total relaxation, the options for visitors are endless.

The beautiful scenery and a magnificent countryside can be seen and enjoyed from a cruiser, from a bicycle or simply by walking the many towpaths and travelling the myriad quiet country roads that surround the seven fascinating waterways of Ireland. The country is a paradise for anglers with an abundance of easily accessible coarse and game fisheries.

You can delve into the fascinating heritage of Ireland, which can be seen in ancient stones and circles, in monastic ruins and grand cathedrals, in stately homes and in the many museums, most of which are accessible from the waterways. If it is excitement you seek, try the canoe rrail on the River Erne or go kayaking on the Barrow. If you wish you can learn to sail, particularly on the Shannon and the Erne systems. In many locations waterskiing and wakeboarding can also be experienced.

The Barrow Navigation – Athy to St Mullins.
The Erne System – Belleck to Belturbet.
The Grand Canal – Dublin to Shannon Harbour. (Naas branch and Barrow line)
The Lower Bann – Barmouth to Lough Neagh.
The Royal Canal – Dublin to Abbeyshrule (under restoration, eventually The Shannon).
The Shannon Erne Waterway – Belturbet to Leitrim.
The Shannon Navigation – Lough Allen/Lough Key to Limerick.

The following pages contain basic cruising details of three popular sections of the Shannon Navigation and the Barrow Navigation.

Above: St John's Lough on the Shannon-Erne Waterway.

Below left: The Grand Canal, Dublin. Waterways Ireland.

Below right: A beautiful scene at Devenish on the Erne system. Waterways Ireland.

The Shannon Navigation
Lough Ree

The River Shannon is more than 200 miles (321.8km) long but it rises only 250ft (76m) above sea level at its highest point, thus making it relatively easy to navigate. This gentle giant of a waterway has only six locks and is arguably Ireland's greatest attraction for cruising enthusiasts. As long ago as 300BC the Romans mapped the river and its various lakes because it was an important early European trading route.

During the first millennium, the Vikings sailed the river, their famous longboats carrying them as far upstream as Lough Ree, where they settled at Rindoon, on a strategic promontory midway between the present-day towns of Athlone and Roscommon.

But even in these modern times, local economies are still dependant upon the water for a large proportion of their income via tourism.

It is possible to travel through a great deal of this magical land by waterway. The newly completed Shannon-Erne link connects the north of Ireland with the River Shannon, while the Grand Canal and the Barrow Navigation connect Dublin with the south-east, and thus the sea at New Ross. Sailing southwards on the Shannon beyond Limerick will take those who have their sights set on wider horizons to the Atlantic Ocean.

The vast Shannon system contains three major lakes (Loughs). Lough Allen to the north and Lough Derg to the south are complemented by the vast expanse of Lough Ree (Ri in Irish) in the Midlands region of the country.

Historically, the town of Athlone was always a place of major strategic importance, standing as it does on a reasonably narrow section of the river to the south of Lough Ree. Many water-borne travellers reach Athlone by the river having cruised either north, south or, indeed, west (via the Grand Canal/Shannon) but increasingly, cruising holidays originating from the town are becoming popular.

The ancient waterside town is only 80 miles (128km) from the ferry ports at Dublin and Dun Laoghaire. It is a town with an abundance of good services.

The twin towers and graceful dome of the Renaissance-style church dedicated to the saints Peter and Paul can be seen from whatever direction you approach the town – by road or water. It has all the appearance of an ancient place of worship but the impressive building was completed in the late 20th century and the first mass held there on St Patrick's Day 1937. Of much greater age is the castle, Norman in origin, adjacent to the river.

Athlone Castle is the oldest surviving building in the town. It dates from 1210 and was built to form a bridgehead across the River Shannon for

Above: Heading off: a typical scene on the big Shannon loughs. Cock-boat in tow and cycles firmly secured to the bow rail.

Top left: Athlone Castle and round tower in the attractive riverside area ajacent to the lock.

Top right: The Hodson Bay harbour near Athlone.

Above left: A typical Lough Ree buoy (channel marker).

Above right: Looking upstream from the lock with the Church of SS Peter and Paul on the left and the Radison on the right.

the Norman invasion of the province of Connaught. It now serves as a museum.

The big attraction to the modern tourist is the nearby lough, which can fairly be described as a small inland sea. This expanse of water has also attracted visitors of a different kind: the Vikings had settlements on, and fought over, the right to dominate Lough Ree. Well before that, the Roman cartographer Ptolemy is said to have mapped the river in 300BC.

From 931-937 there appears to have been a Viking presence on Lough Ree. However, not all those raiders came by water like the warrior Turgesius, who sailed up the Shannon in 796. In what some call the second Viking coming, Olaf Ceancaireach (Olaf the scabby-head) arrived on the lough having carried his longships overland, following a raid on Lough Erne in 936.

There are more than 50 islands on the lough, all of which were investigated by the Vikings. Hare Island was once wealthy and inhabited by monks, and was the home of St Ciaran before he founded the famous monastic site at Clonmacnoise, farther down river. The main islands are Saits (0.82sq km), Inchmore (0.865sq km) and Inchcleraun (0.577sq km). The Nordic invaders are said to have founded Rindoon, on the shore of the lake.

Hundreds of Viking vessels have reputedly sunk in the lough with more than 60 of

Turgesius' fleet suffering that fate in a battle with King Malachy, which allegedly lasted for three months. After that battle the defeated Turgesius was drowned in the nearby Lough Owel by the conquering king. The area has over the years been the location of many great historic finds, which have included several Viking hoards and a great many Celtic and Bronze Age artefacts.

The stranglehold of the Vikings was finally broken in 1014 when they were defeated at the Battle of Clontarf by the High King of Ireland, the legendary Brian Boru. There were two major Viking treasure finds on Hare Island, consisting of gold ingots, bracelets and armbands. In Irish folklore that location is also where the fierce warrior Queen Maeve was killed.

The ancient Celts held their women in high esteem, and in the Celtic nations women shared equal rights with their men. Furthermore Celtic women were not bound by the constraints of monogamy and so it was with Queen Maeve, who was said to have taken '100 lovers' among her followers, thereby ensuring her army's loyalty.

Would you believe that Lough Ree has its own monster? Not to be outdone by their Celtic cousins in Scotland the Irish, it seems, have had reported sightings of an unexplained creature that may inhabit the lough. What's more, the sightings of the serpent-like creature were made by three reliable witnesses.

Priests Father Quigly, Father Murray and Father Burke were all familiar with Lough Ree, which they fished on a regular basis. They were fishing off Holly Point at 9.30pm on 18 May 1960, a warm summery evening. One of them suddenly spotted an unusual object about 100 yards away. Subsequently a report appeared in the local paper.

The *Westmeath Independent* broke the story on 28 May 1960 with front-page headlines stating: 'Lough Ree Monster Sighted!' In an interview with one of the paper's senior reporters, one of the priests stated: "It was moving. It went down under the water and came up again in the form of a loop. The length from the end of the coil to the head was six feet. There was about 18in of head and neck over the water. The head and neck were narrow in comparison to the thickness of a good-sized salmon.

"It was getting its propulsion from underneath the water, and we did not see all of it. There were two sections above the water; a forward section of uniform girth, stretching quite straight out of the water and inclined at the plane of the surface at about 30 degrees, in length about 18-24in. The diameter of this long leading section we would estimate to be about four inches. At its extremity, which we took to be a serpent-like head, it tapered rather abruptly to a point."

In 2001 a Swedish diving team with modern sonar gear attempted to seek out further evidence. Its inconclusive findings only added to the myth.

Lough Ree is the second-largest of the great lakes on the Shannon Navigation and poses an interesting challenge to the cruising fraternity. There are several hire companies in the area and the majority of craft on the lough during the main season (May-October) are hired.

Navigation is not difficult; the main channels on Lough Ree and the surrounding river are well marked. Waterways Ireland has produced an excellent cruising guide and its purchase is recommended. Naturally such a large expanse of water has areas into which it is unadvisable to take a craft of moderate size; those locations are clearly marked both on the charts and on the water with buoys. It is not possible to land on all of the islands on the lough and it is advisable to gain local knowledge before planning to visit one.

Lough Ree is 25km (16 miles) long and varies in width from 11km (seven miles) at it widest point. The average width of the northern region is 3km (two miles) and the southern half 6km (four miles). The lake lies entirely on carboniferous limestone and has an irregular shoreline, populated by extensive reed beds. For the greater part the Lough is shallow and is less than 6m deep. However, there are a number of deep trenches running in a north-south direction, in which soundings of 35m have been taken. The surface area of water is quoted as being 105sq km. Lough Ree is a mixed wild fishery with a good stock of trout, making it popular with anglers.

All photographs by the author.

Below left: Choppy water on the wide expanse of the lough.

Bottom left: There are numerous shoals to be avoided when sailing on Lough Ree.

Below right: A typical River Shannon summer scene as one of the many craft specially designed for hire heads downstream with its happy band of travellers.

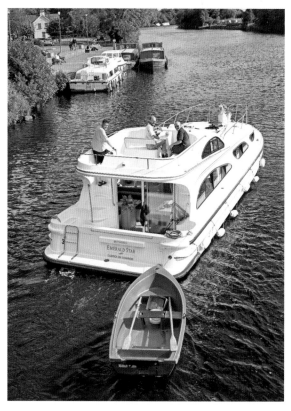

The Shannon Navigation
Athlone to Portumna

Cruising south on the Shannon from the vibrant riverside city of Athlone, you first need to negotiate the town's huge lock but, fear not: it is ably manned by lock keeper Tim Connelly and his helpful team. In the season, 4 April to 26 September, the lock operates between 9am and 8.30pm, Monday to Saturday inclusive, and from 9am to 6pm on Sundays. The very reasonable sum of €6 per vessel is charged.

It is a big lock next to a huge weir and you can expect to be in the company of other craft while using it, often as many as eight boats. If you are travelling upstream, be sure not to miss the last lock as there are but a few mooring places below the town.

On leaving the town, the river flows almost at an instant through a change of landscape, and one that is quite different from that surrounding Lough Ree upstream. You are heading into flat meadowland and sailing on through The Callows, a vast area of watermeadows. Bounded by the reedbeds on the banks of the river and extending in all directions, they start as rolling green pasture and hayfields, which seem to go on forever, and end as valuable peatland.

It is a great centre for naturalists, both in summer, when the corncrake can be heard, and in winter, when thousands of wild duck and wading birds congregate in the flood plain. This is also good angling country – fish of 20lb or more are common and there is no rod licence required for coarse or pike fishing on the River Shannon or Lough Ree.

The river on this section is broad and sweeps majestically along. It is ideal territory for the cruising novice to be given charge of the boat as the channel is clearly marked and forward vision is unobstructed for mile after mile.

Peacefully cruising through the meadows of Co Oflay towards Shannonbridge, you may get the feeling that you are passing through a very special place. And you are. The ancient monastic site of Clonmacnoise is about to come into view and those who see it from the river for their first time will never forget it.

Clomnacnoise is situated on a ridge overlooking a large area of bog from which the River Shannon picks up colouration as it flows by. This ancient religious site dates back almost 1500 years. It was founded by St Ciaran, the son of an Ulsterman who settled in the province of Connaught.

It is easy to see why he chose the site for his monastery. Strategically it made good sense dominating, as it does, the surrounding flatlands for miles around and being protected on one side by the mighty river, which in 545AD was very important. It was at the central meeting place of river and road travel in Celtic Ireland. The location borders the three provinces of Connaught, Munster and Leinster.

The monastery is on the east side of the River Shannon, in what was then the Kingdom of Meath, but occupying a position so central it was the burial place of many of the kings of Connaught as well as those of Tara.

Shortly after his arrival, Ciaran met Prince Diarmuid, who helped him to build the first church – a small wooden structure and the first of many small churches to be clustered on the site. Diarmuid was to be crowned the first Christian High King of Ireland. He did not live to see his

Above: Shannonbridge. The Old Fort and 1757-built bridge are passed by the very smart Dutch-built cruiser *Liberty III* as she heads south for Lough Derg.

Below: JJ Hough's Bar at Banagher.

monastery grow and flourish… he died aged 33 of yellow plague just four years after settling.

The monastery attracted many of the scholars of Ireland and farther afield and it was to become the most illustrious school in Europe. No single large church exists, or ever existed, at Clonmacnoise; instead there were a number of small churches of simple plan and originally of wooden construction.

Standing on the site now is a cluster of ruined churches, most of which date from the 12th century onwards, and they are within a graveyard. The monastic settlement has been subjected to many violent and destructive acts and it was destroyed by fire on at least 13 occasions. Each time the monks diligently rebuilt their settlement. In 1552 it was finally reduced to ruin by the English garrison in Athlone and from that time onwards there were no monasteries in Ireland for almost 300 years.

The stone used for the famous north and south crosses on the site was transported to the spot by river from the Bernagh Mountains on the shore of Lough Derg to the south. There are seven churches within the boundary of Clonmacnoise and some local people even call it Seven Churches. It has been under painstaking restoration by Ireland's Office of Public Works for some time and it now has an established and manned visitor centre.

The ancient monastic site is about 12 miles from Athlone, and words cannot fully describe its Celtic beauty, let alone begin to explain its mystical and religious significance. Suffice it to say, there are landing stages at Clonmacnoise; sailing straight by them without stopping for a while would truly be your loss.

From the truly sublime to… well, use your own word to describe it. The next structure to dominate the river as you journey south is the huge power station at Shannonbridge. Not only can you not fail to see it you are sure to smell it, for the generating station is peat-fired. The aroma may be loved by most and even hated by some but it is a truly Irish one and always puts me in mind of malt whiskey. That in itself is a good enough reason to stop and sample the many delights of Shannonbridge.

The town has a splendid bridge over the Shannon that was constructed as long ago as 1757 and is still in use. During Napoleonic times the British heavily fortified the town and the fort is today a restaurant that still stands resplendent on the west bank of the river. Waterways Ireland installed a collection of new jetties upstream from the bridge in 2003 so visiting cruisers are well catered for.

The next town of note on the downstream

Above left: Cruising between Banagher and Meelick Lock.

Above right: When sailing the Shannon you will inevitably share the river with other users, some going a lot faster than you are. However, there is plenty of room for all.

Below: The wide expanse of the river below Meelick is illustrated in this panoramic picture.

journey is the riverside town of Banagher, a location that simply brims with Irish history. Banagher, which means 'ford of the rocks', was originally a small port in the 18th century. It was once home to such literary greats as Anthony Trollope and Charlotte Bronte, and also to William Wilde, the father of the great Oscar. A strategic river-crossing for more than 600 years, Banagher today is a place of peace and beauty. Over the past 50 years it has grown in importance as a visitor centre.

The town is centred on its main street, which runs downhill to the river and harbour. There is a well-appointed harbour below the bridge and, although in season individual moorings can be at a premium, 'doubling up' is well worth it if only for a night-time trip to JJ Hough's (pronounced Hocks), a tavern with a character of its own.

That hostelry does not just have character, it is peopled by them. The delightful boss, Jack Hough, often entertains his customers with a ditty or two, occasionally accompanied by his very talented son on the bodhran, a traditional goatskin one-sided drum. The Irish word 'bodhar' means deaf or haunting. It stirs the spirit when played with either a 'tipper' or beater, and sometimes is played with the bare hand.

However, the greatest treat of all in 'Hocks' (and long may it continue to be so) is the lovely Teresa with her unique style of piano and vocals and her amazing rendition of Enjoy Yourself (It's Later Than You Think). She can (and nightly

does) entertain a mixed crowd of Europeans and leave them simply wanting more. It's compliment enough when setting off from the quay the following day to hear Teresa's signature tune being sung in all sorts of accents. Priceless!

On the journey south, the awesome beauty of Lough Derg is in prospect but first there is Meelick Lock to be negotiated. That facility is in the capable hands of lock keeper Stephen McGarry, and it is open for the same periods as Athlone and, indeed, all other Shannon locks and bridges.

The next town encountered is Portumna, an important cruiser base for the Emerald Star Line. Situated at the head of Lough Derg (which many say is the most attractive lake of the Shannon system), Portumna is a significant centre for angling.

There are several ancient ruins, mostly of religious foundations. However, the remains of one of the last castles to be built in Ireland are at Derryhiveny, about three miles from the town.

Portumna Castle was a great semi-fortified house built before 1618 by Richard Burke, 4th Earl of Clanricarde. It was the main seat of that family for more than 200 years, until it was gutted by fire in 1826. The ground floor of the house is now open to the public.

As far as river travellers going south are concerned, the swing bridge over the N65 at Portumna is the gateway to Lough Derg.

All photographs by the author.

Below left: Tim Connelly, the friendly lock keeper at Athlone, lends a helping hand to this boater.

Below Right: The magical sight of Clonmacnoise (Seven Churches) seen from the river.

Bottom left: You are likely to see many and varied types of craft on the Shannon.

Bottom right: In hot pursuit? The Garda riverboat seen travelling between Athlone and Shannonbridge.

The Shannon Navigation
Lough Derg

Continuing to cruise south on the mighty River Shannon, the swing bridge at Portumna is considered by many to be the gateway to serenity for beyond it lies the awe-inspiring and mysterious Lough Derg. Setting off south for the first time, the unwary traveller might not at first realise the significance of an instruction, sometimes given. "Be sure to call and see the two fellas!" "Who, what fellas?" you may ask. "Sure, Terry and Garry. Good luck. Have a safe sail." Maybe all will become obvious later.

Lough Derg is without a doubt one of Ireland's greatest lakes, and many who have sailed there consider it to be the most beautiful. Yet it can, except possibly for peak weeks in the high season, be one of the Shannon Navigation's least-used places and is a truly tranquil location. To sail towards the centre of a 32,000 acre lake, which is almost 25 miles (40km) long, and to be the only craft in sight is quite something!

It really is possible to feel totally alone on this vast body of water, which really does have all the attributes of an inland sea. At its deepest points it can be plumbed to a depth of more than 100ft (30 metres) and there are more than 200km of navigable waterways emanating from it. The entrance for those travelling south is Portumna and the southern extremity of the lake is marked by the conjoined Shannonside towns of Killaloe and Ballina. Lough Derg is skirted by three counties: Galway, North Tipperary and Clare.

Before continuing, let us put the record straight: there is another Lough Derg in Ireland and that body of water is situated in Co Donegal. It is a relatively small lake but is of great religious significance. In that water there is an islet known as Station Island, more popularly called St Patrick's Purgatory. The islet has been a place of pilgrimage since ancient times. Traditionally the pilgrimages are three-day affairs held during the period June 1-August 15 annually. Loch Dearg in Irish has the meaning 'red lake'.

Lough Derg, in keeping with the whole of the Shannon Navigation, is famous for its huge stock of fish and is said by some to be the best-mixed fishery in Ireland. It is particularly rich in wild trout, the taste of which when freshly grilled has to be tried to be believed.

Coarse species like pike and bream are plentiful in the lake's depths; tench and rudd are to be found in and around its numerous weed beds. Lough Derg eels, very much a delicacy and once sold as such at London's Billingsgate Fish Market, can also be tempted to take a carefully offered bait.

Lough Derg provides rich habitats for a diverse flora. Its northern shores are more species-rich as the limestone underfoot provides suitable soils. Here the Irish fleabane (Inula salicina), unknown elsewhere in Ireland or Britain, flourishes on some rocky shores and islands. With willow-shaped and toothed leaves, its yellow sunflower heads are quite distinctive in July and August.

Above: Having been released by the opening of the swing bridge carrying the N65 road, these craft head away from Portumna and into the open waters of Lough Derg.

The mix of deep and shallow waters, together with reed beds, marsh and rocky shoreline, provides habitats for a variety of plants such as the water lilies of the deep waters; the rare flowering rush of the shallows; hemp agrimony of the reed beds; the rushes themselves, many types of grasses and sedges in the marsh lands; and buckthorn, dogwood, spindle and Irish whitebeam on the rocky shores. On the southern shores of the lake the waterfront soil turns acidic and plant life is less abundant.

Most of Ireland's larger wild animals can be found around Lough Derg. Some, like the rabbit, hare, grey squirrel, stoat and mink, are active during the day while others like the hedgehog, badger and otter are nocturnal creatures. The fox is most often seen at dawn or dusk and they are evident in big numbers. Fallow deer are now very much part of Portumna Forest Park. The pine marten is now being seen in greater numbers.

The Shannon system is perhaps unequalled in Europe for the quality of its bird life, and Lough Derg shares in this distinction. The avian visitors include coot, moorhen, grebe, duck, heron, gull, kingfisher, cormorant, bunting, mute swan, warblers, swifts, swallows and house martins.

The main channels on Lough Derg are clearly marked but you would be unwise to venture forth on to this vast lake without an up-to-date Waterways Ireland navigation chart.

In rougher weather perhaps only experienced mariners should consider sailing Lough Derg. The wind (as on most big expanses of water) can blow strongly, creating more than a bit of a swell. Such conditions can make passages in smaller craft uncomfortable, so the best advice is to try to make your voyage within sight of other vessels.

Nature is wonderful to behold and embrace up close but she can be a hard taskmistress, so don't take chances. But have no fear if, for an hour or three, you choose not to sail. There are plenty of lakeside hostelries in which to wait for the weather to turn.

Above left: The delightful first view of the enclosed harbour section first afforded to sailers at Garrykennedy.

Above right: Night time at Garrykennedy.

Below left: The plaque on the remains of Garrykennedy Castle.

Below right: The inner harbour at Garrykennedy, complete with its ruined castle.

GARRYKENNEDY CASTLE WAS ONE OF MANY ERECTED ON THE SHORES OF LOUGH DERG DURING THE PERIOD 1450 - 1600 A.D. THESE CASTLES, (OR TOWER HOUSES) WERE BUILT FOR DEFENCE BY IMPORTANT LOCAL LAND OWNERS SUCH AS BUTLER, O KENNEDYS,O BRIEN OF ARRA. GARRYKENNEDY CASTLE IS REFERRED TO IN THE CIVIL SURVEY OF 1654 A.D. AS THE DEMOLISHED CASTLE OF CASTLEGARE AND TWO CENTURIES LATER AS SLANGER CASTLE. JOHN O'DONOVAN ESTIMATED THE DIMENSIONS OF THE RUIN IN 1840 AT 17' BY 11' AND 40 IN HEIGHT. MUCH OF THE STONE FROM THE CASTLE WAS USED TO CONSTRUCT THE EXISTING HARBOUR SO THE SKILLS OF THE MEDIEVAL CRAFTSMEN ARE STILL UTILISED BY THE PEOPLE TODAY

It is not advisable to hug the shore or, indeed, sail close to as, in many cases, that is precisely where any danger from underwater shoals might be lurking. Follow the chart and stick to the rules of navigation and all will be well.

The marked navigation channels are well out near the centre of the lake and that may, of course, be where the highest winds can be found. For all people, not just youngsters and non-swimmers, life jackets are an essential to have on board, and they should preferably be worn at all times. A working mobile phone is a safety aid familiar to all so, in addition, be sure you know the appropriate local numbers.

Lough Derg is very much a lake of myth; both it and the surrounding area are steeped in history. Its shores have been settled since prehistoric times and its main channel is part of one of Ireland's oldest trade routes. In medieval times hermits, heroes, soldiers, raiders, students and pilgrims journeyed from the Atlantic Ocean to the Irish Midlands by way of this water highway. Norse raiders, too, sailed its waters and left their mark.

Near the centre of the lake is a small, now uninhabited, island, a place that had great importance attached to it in early Christian times. It is called Inis Cealtra or Holy Island. In its time it boasted a monastery dating from the 7th century and no less than five churches and other buildings, including an 80ft tall round tower. There is also an ancient cemetery. The island lies nearly half-a-mile from the mainland and one-and-a-half miles (2km) from Mountshannon.

The 50-acre island proved irresistible to the Viking marauders and its religious buildings were robbed and pillaged by them on at least two occasions. It is still possible to land on the island, which has been a place of pilgrimage for over 1000 years.

Nearby Tuamgraney, on the East Clare shore, has what is reputed to be the oldest church still in use in the British Isles. St Cronan's Church dates from 950, when it was built to replace a 7th century monastery.

No self-respecting Irish lough would be without a spooky tale or two and this great expanse of water is no exception. There is 'Finn the monster killer', a legendary Celtic hero who supposedly killed a huge monster that had crawled from the lake in order to terrify the locals. Finn sliced open the great ogre with a

Above left: Killaloe and its fine stone bridge seen from the town quay at Ballina.

Above right: Looking back upstream from the bridge at Ballina – truly '40 shades of green' country!

Below: The wall of the canal (to Limerick) at Killaloe provides good moorings.

mighty sword and, in doing so, released 200 men who had been trapped in the beast's belly. But he might also have set free a smaller monster in doing so. According to legend, that creature slithered back into the water. It is said to still live in Lough Derg.

There is also the fire-breathing hound of Castle Biggs, and an abomination with cloven hooves, supposedly protecting a hidden horde of treasure. Edmond Roe O'Kennedy was murdered in the 16th century without first revealing the location of his treasure hoard. His spectre, complete with bleeding throat, has been said to appear at Annagh Castle.

To cap it all there is said to be a phantasmal vessel seen 'always travelling in a northerly direction with gentle rhythmical singing emanating from it'. Some say, tongue in cheek, that it has to be the combined wandering spirits of all the Welsh rugby supporters whose teams have suffered defeat at the hands of their Celtic cousins.

The wags on the bridge at Portumna were referring to the delightful waterside communities of Terryglass and Garrykennedy. Both villages have well-appointed harbours with excellent facilities and no shortage of suitable watering-holes.

Terryglass is in Co Tipperary and it is the first harbour on that bank of the lough. It can be reached shortly after entering the lake at Portumna. It is a charming village that has won numerous tidy town awards and is a very popular place. The harbour at Terryglass is quite modern but still lends itself to a friendly, sociable atmosphere.

The village proper is a short walk away but it is a delight and well worth the easy effort. There are two pubs in the village sitting side-by-side and both are renowned for good food, music and craic. There is also a well-stocked village store and post office. The village is the site of a 6th century monastic settlement, of which only a small part remains. St Colman founded a monastery there and it became an important centre for learning.

The Book of Leinster, which can now be seen in Trinity College, Dublin, was produced there. It is a historically important document that contains tales and poems from the Middle Ages in Ireland. There is one remaining wall from the abbey in the village and a spring, said to have healing properties, can be found nearby. The Vikings frequently raided the abbey, and it was burnt to the ground in 1264.

The history of Garrykennedy, Co Tipperary, dates back to the Norman era, when the village was the stronghold of the O'Kennedys. The ruins of their castle (dating from 1480) on the lakeshore are the centrepiece of the modern-day village. Garrykennedy has only a small harbour area and accordingly there is a very friendly atmosphere. It is common to see cruisers mooring up against the high stone wall beneath the ruins of the castle.

There is a well-signed walk in the lakeside Woodland Park and the main street is literally only a stone's throw away. The tiny village has two pubs with restaurants and both are famous for their traditional music and good food. Up to the 1950s it was a busy port with regular visits by the Guinness barges delivering barrels of stout. An interesting item is the village letterbox, which illustrates the transition from British jurisdiction to that of the Saorstá (Free State) post. It dates from 1922.

Around the Lough there are, of course, several other places that can be listed in the must-see category: Droominier has the third-oldest yacht club in the world (1837) and, on the Clare shore, Scariff village is accessible to boaters from the Graney River. There is also Cahir Island and close by the ruins of Ballykelly Castle. Whitegate and Mountshannon are also on that same shore, and all these locations have delights of their own.

As you sail on south the landscape is

Above left: The outer harbour at Garrykennedy.

Above right: You will see all kinds of craft on the Shannon. This Dutch barge-style craft is about to berth at Terryglass beside a supercruiser.

dominated by splendid mountains which seem to cup the lake within their verdant hands. On the Clare shoreline are the distant Slieve Aughty Mountains and farther south the Slieve Bernagh Hills. On the Tipperary side the Arra Mountains dominate, especially when the Lough begins to narrow as the Shannon Navigation becomes a river again and flows towards the sea. Next are the delightful linked towns of Killaloe and Ballina.

Travelling south (downstream), Killaloe is on the right bank and therefore in Co Clare, while across the splendid 13-arched stone bridge and on the left bank is Ballina, in Co Tipperary. There are mooring facilities on both sides but the newly constructed quay at Ballina is often the easiest at which to gain a berth. The two historic towns are ideal as stopover places where pubs, shops and restaurants abound. Just upstream of the town there is a relatively new marina.

The area has strong historical connections. Killaloe has a 13th century cathedral (St Flannan's). Immediately inside the entrance to it is a romanesque doorway from an earlier church. The stone standing before the doorway is unique for its ogham and runic inscriptions. One, a Viking runic inscription, reads 'Thorgrim carved this stone'; the other, carved in ancient ogham, asks for 'a blessing upon Thorgrim'.

Killaloe's greatest claim to historical fame is as the site of Kincora, the palace of Brian Boru, the 11th century High King of Ireland. Brian Boru's royal residence stood on the summit of the hill, above the bridge at Killaloe. He lived there from 1002 to 1014 and the residence probably covered the site now occupied by the Catholic church, the village green and some neighbouring houses.

Located northwards from Killaloe are the remains of Brian Boru's Fort (Beal Boru). Little more than the actual site has survived and it is marked by traces of earthen ramparts and a surrounding ditch. The fort environs are of considerable antiquity; traces of Bronze Age occupation have been found.

Killaloe is the downstream starting-point for a canalised section of the river that leads to Limerick. The town was once a busy steamer port with regular services, and the Inland Steam Navigation Company had their headquarters on the quayside and their craft made two return sailings daily to Limerick. From Killaloe passengers could travel north by steamer to Shannon Harbour and then on to Dublin in canal packets via the Grand Canal.

All photographs by the author.

Above left: Cruising gently upstream after overnighting in Killaloe.

Above right: South of France? No, South of Ireland! The skipper of *Liberty III* enjoys a spot of July sunshine.

Below left: With its sail down and under power, this small craft has just crossed from Scarriff and is seen approaching Terryglass.

Below right: The swing bridge at Portumna. A green light for the downstream travellers.

Ireland's hidden waterway treasure
the magical River Barrow

It is known in Ireland as one of The Three Sisters, the other two ladies being the River Suir and the River Nore. The Barrow is the longest and most prominent of the three and is the second-longest river in Ireland. It is just over 119 miles long (192km), the navigable waterway is 42.25 miles long (68km), and it has several canalised sections and 23 Victorian-style locks.

The Shannon waterway is home to all types of craft ranging from narrow boats to sea-going cruisers and sailing boats. On the other hand, the Barrow system and, in particular, its middle and upper reaches, is very definitely suitable only for powered craft that fall into either the small cruiser or narrow boat category – length 18.5m (61ft), beam 3.9m (12.75ft) and their draft in summer can be as low as 0.76m (2.5ft).

The present-day Barrow Navigation begins at Athy in Co Kildare and has a junction just above the town (via the Barrow Line) with the Grand Canal, in the quiet rural area of Vicarstown. The Grand Canal, arguably Ireland's most important man-made waterway, was built between 1756 and 1803 and links Dublin on the east coast to the River Shannon. In its heyday the canal carried both passengers and goods such as peat and coal. However, the two most important goods carried were grain and water, used by the Guinness brewery to make its famous porter.

The Barrow Navigation ends just beyond the attractive and religiously significant village of St Mullins in South Carlow. That area nestles between the Blackstairs Mountains on one side

Above: Looking downstream towards Muine Bheag, aka Bagenalstown, the river tumbles over the weir to the right while the cut continues past the old canalside grain stores.

and Brandon Hill on the other, and the Barrow River flows along the valley floor between those pleasant and wooded hills. At the end of the navigation, the Barrow becomes tidal for the remainder of its journey to the sea, via first the Barrow Estuary and then Waterford Harbour.

In 1703 a committee was set up in the Irish House of Commons in order to prepare a Parliamentary Bill for the cutting of 'various navigations' needed in order to make the river navigable for trade. There was a delay of a little over 60 years before work on the system began and the 10 separate navigations (lateral sections of canal) were completed in 1800.

However, the lack of consistent depth of water in the river sections caused problems, especially in summer, and commercial traffic was often disrupted.

A fatal blow to the waterway's commercial future was delivered in 1935 when a drainage scheme actually silted up of some of the lateral canals. Almost certainly as a direct result, commercial trade ended on the system in 1959.

Barrow Navigation has, by comparison to the Shannon, continued to be a tranquil and relatively forgotten waterway. It really is worth discovering and is, in comparison to British inland waterway cruising, very different!

The lateral canal sections are relatively clear and can normally be travelled safely although, to the uninitiated observer, they may have the appearance of being unused. The gin-clear waters of the Barrow Navigation are safe to swim in, say the Irish authorities. These

unspoiled, unpolluted and peaceful areas of waterway must be among the best in Europe.

The town of Athy was the site of an ancient and much-used river crossing; the town's name literally means 'ford of Ae'. The town once had two castles nearby, Whites and Woodstock, the former having been built in 1506 by the eighth Earl of Kildare and the latter dating from the mid-13th century. Allegedly, during a fire at Woodstock Castle, an infant was rescued by a monkey and thereafter the Kildares included a chimpanzee on their coat of arms.

On leaving the town of Athy (south), boaters should take the Levistown Cut, which is a two-mile lateral canal and is the longest on the navigation. This cut runs alongside the main R417 road to Carlow and was dug to avoid an otherwise unnavigable stretch of the river.

On the east bank is Grangemellon Castle, which was once the home of 'Handsome Jack' St Leger, founder of the famous St Leger horse race and prominent in the infamous Hellfire Club. Members reputedly took part in mock religious ceremonies and used masks and costumes to allow them to indulge secretly in varying degrees of debauchery.

Shortly after passing the castle, craft rejoin the river proper after negotiating Levistown Lock.

After the Barrow passes through Maganey Lock, the River Greese joins it, as does the River Lerr in the vicinity of Shurle Castle. The next navigational aid of importance is the marker to Bestfield Cut which is not, given the natural growth according to season, always easy to see. After Bestfield Lock there is then a clear run to the city of Carlow, a splendidly solid old town besieged by Cromwell in 1650.

Worthy of mention is the story that Bestfield Lock, and the immediate area surrounding it, is said to be haunted. Boaters have reported strange and unexplained knocking sounds on the hulls of their craft while moored for the night.

There is another lateral canal downstream from Carlow – and Clogrennan Cut is another that is easily missed and so is clearly marked. The only natural weir on the Barrow system is at Cloggrenna, and the castle ruins nearby are worth a visit. The next place of note is Milford, where stands the old mill once used as a generating plant for Carlow's street lights.

Leighlinbridge, which is passed next, is an attractive and welcoming township. It's seven-arched bridge is really a rather special one, built in 1320 and then attractively widened (but only, it seems, to allow the passage of nothing more than fat horses!) in 1789.

This historic place has a good selection of welcoming hostelries such as the Lord Bagenal Inn, a family-run hotel with a mouth-watering range of to tempt any palate. At the rear is a

Above left: A family of swans enjoy their tranquil surroundings.

Above right: The lateral cut has the look of a lush rain forest pool as it skirts past Bagenalstown. The wall of the elongated weir can be seen in line with the small green island while the river can be glimpsed through the bushes on the right of the view.

Below left and right: The oldest bridge on the Barrow system at Leighlinbridge, built in 1320 and widened in 1789. The left-most arches lead to the cut while the three on the right are in line with the river proper and the new marina and berthing facility to the rear of the Lord Bagenal Inn.

Ireland's hidden waterway treasure: the magical River Barrow | 107

small marina located just off the main channel of the river. It is worth staying until after dark if only to appreciate the floodlit beauty of the bridge and the ruins of Black Castle.

The next town on the journey downstream is called by its Gaelic name, Muine Bheag. It was alternatively named Bagenalstown in the 18th century after Walter Bagenal, who settled there and dreamed of creating a second Versailles. In 1970 the townspeople voted to retain the town's Gaelic name. Accordingly the sign on the railway station andsome buildings reads Muine Bheag; many road signs and most local folk in conversation still call it Bagenalstown.

The river now passes through very fertile country with neatly cultivated fields and pasture land below the backdrop of the Blackstairs Mountains and Mount Leinster, as Goresbridge is reached. The splendid Brandon Hill dominates the view to the west as you glide under a fine specimen of a nine-arch bridge, built in 1756.

Farther on there is a particularly delightful stretch of the river that has the area surrounding Borris Demesne on its lush east bank. The river then becomes pinched on either side by sloping banks thick in foliage and trees, particularly around Clashganna, and there is a profusion of

Above left: The bridge over the river connecting two counties – on the right Graignamhagh in Kilkenny and on the left Tinnahinch in Carlow.

Above right: The lock below the town of Graignamhagh on the cut at Tinnahinch. Note that the paddles are set into the gates.

Below left: A secluded stretch of the Barrow Navigation near Bagenalstown, aka Muine Bheag.

Below right: Below the lock at Milford (looking upstream), the river is to the right and the lock mouth leading to the cut is to the left.

ancient sandstone boulders to be seen.

Ballykeenan Lock is reached soon after. As well as being the narrowest and deepest on the navigation, it is the only one with a double chamber.

The town of Graignamahagh in Co Kilkenny is reached next, and it also has a seven-arched bridge, built in 1767 at the same time as the navigation was constructed. This attractive crossing is also floodlit at night and links the town with Tinnahinch in Co Carlow, which is on the eastern bank. The lock to the last navigable section of the Barrow Navigation is situated just downstream (south) from the bridge.

Cruising downstream after the lock, the river valley gradually becomes deeper and it is lined with colourful tiers of trees and dense undergrowth. This type of vista can be enjoyed all the way to St Mullins and, on reaching that location, you are then at the end of the magical Barrow Navigation.

There's only one thing to do: turn round and do it again in the other direction. You will be glad you did.

All photographs by the author.

Inland Waterways Association
of Ireland

Campaigning for
conservation & development

For membership details contact
Brenda Ainsworth 00352(0) 872096353
Or join online at www.iwai.ie

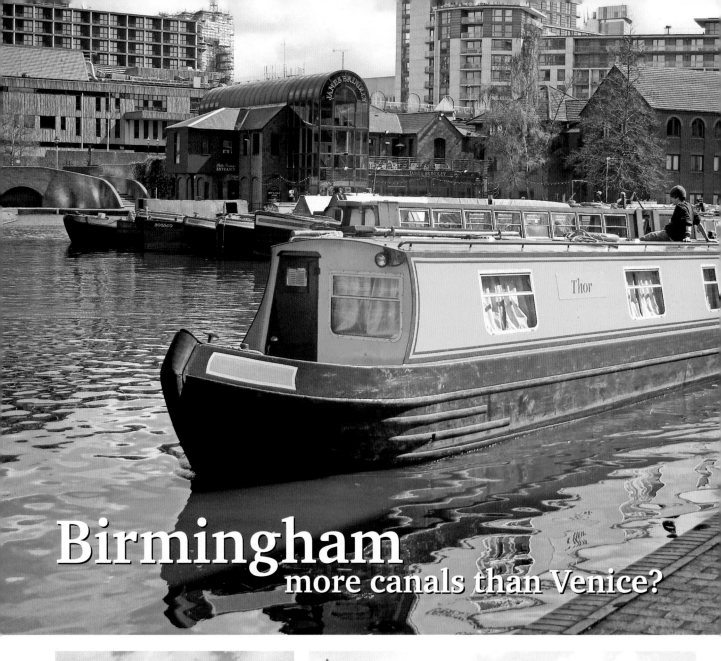

Birmingham
more canals than Venice?

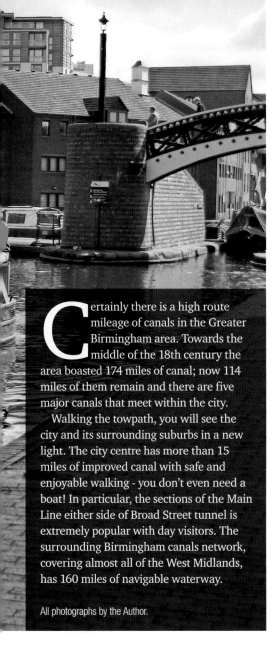

Certainly there is a high route mileage of canals in the Greater Birmingham area. Towards the middle of the 18th century the area boasted 174 miles of canal; now 114 miles of them remain and there are five major canals that meet within the city.

Walking the towpath, you will see the city and its surrounding suburbs in a new light. The city centre has more than 15 miles of improved canal with safe and enjoyable walking - you don't even need a boat! In particular, the sections of the Main Line either side of Broad Street tunnel is extremely popular with day visitors. The surrounding Birmingham canals network, covering almost all of the West Midlands, has 160 miles of navigable waterway.

All photographs by the Author.

Cast iron troughs mounted on stone pillars at Pontcysyllte.

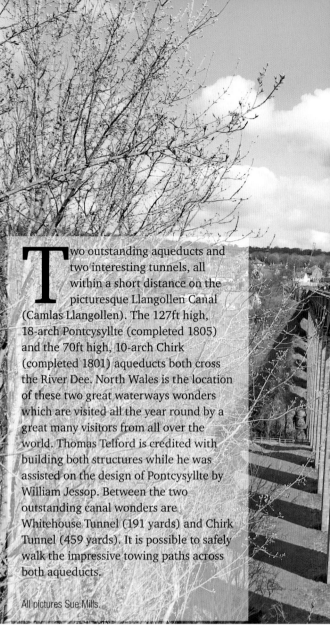

Two outstanding aqueducts and two interesting tunnels, all within a short distance on the picturesque Llangollen Canal (Camlas Llangollen). The 127ft high, 18-arch Pontcysyllte (completed 1805) and the 70ft high, 10-arch Chirk (completed 1801) aqueducts both cross the River Dee. North Wales is the location of these two great waterways wonders which are visited all the year round by a great many visitors from all over the world. Thomas Telford is credited with building both structures while he was assisted on the design of Pontcysyllte by William Jessop. Between the two outstanding canal wonders are Whitehouse Tunnel (191 yards) and Chirk Tunnel (459 yards). It is possible to safely walk the impressive towing paths across both aqueducts.

All pictures Sue Mills.

Pontcysyllte-Chirk

Panoramic view of Pontcysyllte aqueduct.

The 'stream in the sky'.

The look says it all; we have just crossed Pontcysyllte for the first time!

Chirk Tunnel, in which it is possible to walk the towpath.

The all-stone construction of Chirk Aqueduct.

⋀ Ffestiniog Travel

www.festtravel.co.uk

SEE THE WORLD BY RAIL

Escorted, Unescorted and Tailor-made Holidays
Over 30 years' experience

Let Ffestiniog Travel take the worry away and organise a holiday especially for you. Our holidays are designed for people who like to travel by train on famous and not so famous railways of the world. Sit back and relax, enjoy the wonderful scenery and arrive at your destination without a care in the world.

Our brochure describes the excellent tours to Europe and beyond. The holidays are escorted by experienced tour leaders but they are not regimented in any way. Free days are usually included in the itineraries whereby you can go as you please, often armed with a rail pass so that you can explore at your leisure.

We also like to visit exotic places and often ride on trains where individuals cannot travel.

We include scenery, culture and wildlife too. The ultimate train travel experience!

Many of our tours can commence on dates that you select if you would prefer not to travel in a group. Our tailor-made service allows you to choose your destinations. We will arrange airline tickets, train tickets, hotel accommodation and car hire - a complete package just for you.

Harbour Station, Porthmadog, Gwynedd LL49 9NF
Ask for a brochure: tel: 01766 512400
select option 3.
Email: info@festtravel.co.uk

AiTO
THE ASSOCIATION
OF INDEPENDENT
TOUR OPERATORS

Scottish Inland
Waterways Association

Scotland's voice on inland waterways

For membership details contact
Liza Coates 0131 447 5372
www.siwa.org

Droitwich Canals
creating a new cruising ring by 2009

The town of Droitwich Spa has a history firmly entrenched in the waterways. Vines Park, in the centre of the town, has great historical significance as the point where one of the oldest canals in England, the Barge Canal, meets one of the youngest, the Junction Canal. The town came to prominence during the salt trade in the 18th century. Its salt was regarded as a speciality and the town's unique barge, the *Wych*, transported the important mineral from the Midlands to Bristol, where it continued its journey around the UK and abroad.

Railways, coupled with the collapse of the salt trade, led to the decline of the canal industry in the town. The last barge to navigate its way down the canal did so in the 1930s. Today it is not even possible to walk the full length of either the Droitwich Junction or the Barge canals. This restoration project will open up the redundant canal route creating a 7.5-mile (12km) waterway, a linear park to be enjoyed by all. In addition, the restored waterway will link the River Severn with the Worcester and Birmingham Canal, thus generating a new, 21-mile cruising ring.

Much of the original course of the Droitwich Junction Canal between the town and Hanbury

Above: Idyllic is the term that comes to mind; this is an oasis-like section of the abandoned and partly overgrown Droitwich Barge Canal at Ladywood Lock No1. But, for the present, the narrow boat is going nowhere. Author.

Right: Who can fail to see that the delightful Vines Park area will become an instant hit with boaters once the canal links are restored?

is now hard to discern, having been filled in and built over at several locations. To overcome these problems, part of the regeneration of the 'new' waterway will involve a short section of the adjacent River Salwarpe being made navigable – an interesting and practical compromise.

The engineer James Brindley designed the Droitwich Barge Canal, which opened in 1771. It was 5.8 miles (9.3km) long and was a broad beam canal (14 ft) with eight locks. It saw its last boat traffic in 1918, being officially abandoned in 1939. This cut saw one of the earliest uses of a swing bridge.

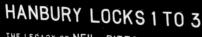

The Droitwich Junction Canal, classified as narrow beam (7ft), was built in 1854 by R Boddington. It was 1.5 miles (2.4km) long with seven locks. When opened it linked the Worcester & Birmingham Canal with the Barge Canal. It was abandoned in 1939, having seen its last working boat in 1920.

Major points of the project.

- 16 locks restored (including four new locks)
- 12km of waterway created, of which 1km will be new cut and 500m canalised river
- 14,800 cu m of silt removed through dredging
- One major bridge construction across A449
- M5 crossing
- 5.6ha of offline reed-bed created (3.1ha net gain)

The benefits are many. The creation of this 21-mile (33.5km) cruising ring means the area is likely to see an increased annual visitor spend of more than £3-million with a possible

Above left: The River Salwarpe to the right of the Barge Lock (the end of the Barge Canal) in Vines Park, Droitwich. This stretch will be the commencement of the new canalised section, which will form the town portion of the newly created Junction Canal. Author.

Above right: Looking towards Droitwich from No 3 lock on the Droitwich Juction Canal, just after its confluence with the Worcester & Birmingham Canal. Above the centre of the lock gates and on the horizon, Droitwich Church can be seen and from that the direction and distance of the newly proposed cut can be judged. Author.

Left: Part of the River Salwarpe, which will be converted to become a canal, is pictured as it leaves the town of Droitwich. The disused tunnel portal on the right marks the original route followed by the Junction Canal on its way to join the Worcester & Birmingham Canal at the nearby Hanbury Junction. Author.

500,000 additional yearly visitor days being created. A study predicts the creation of almost 200 full-time jobs as a result of the scheme and expects that more than 3500 new boat movements-a-year will result. There will also be the creation of 87 permanent moorings and as many as 15 new businesses set up in order to service the predicted visitor numbers. All of this is expected to lead to a 20 per cent increase in usage of the River Severn and the Worcester & Birmingham Canal.

The five partners – The Waterways Trust, British Waterways, Droitwich Canals Trust, Wychavon District Council and Worcestershire County Council – stated that the regeneration work, costing almost £12-million, was set to commence in early 2006. Restoration was expected to be complete by the end of 2008, in time for the 2009 boating season. **W**

Above: Lock No 2 on the Barge Canal – a truly tranquil scene with the pounds between the locks having become almost isolated ponds that attract the wildlife. Author.

Above right: One of the many tasks that face those undertaking canal restoration programmes is clearing Mother Nature's very thorough reclamation work. This grown-over portion of the Droitwich Junction Canal illustrates that point. Author.

Right: The Barge Canal locks were unusual inasmuch as they have four gates and, in the case of the lower gates of Lock 1, are even more different. Note the W-shaped beams on top of the gates in order to allow opening without fouling the road alongside. Author.

Canal cruising rings

A look at the map of the UK inland waterways shows that a large number of cruises can be made using circular routes and that is often an attractive proposition to boaters. Listed are just 10 popular cruising rings.

Avon Ring: 109 miles
Worcester & Birmingham Canal, River Severn, River Avon, Stratford-upon-Avon Canal.

Birmingham Ring: 76 miles
Birmingham & Fazeley Canal, Coventry Canal, Trent & Mersey Canal, Staffordshire & Worcestershire Canal, BCN Main Line Canals.

Cheshire Ring: 95 miles
Bridgewater Canal, Rochdale Canal, Ashton, Peak Forest and Macclesfield Canals, Trent & Mersey Canal.

Four Counties Ring: 110 miles
The Trent & Mersey Canal, Staffordshire & Worcestershire Canal, Shropshire Union Main Line, Shropshire Union – Middlewich Branch.

London Ring: 44 miles
The Grand Union Main Line, Grand Union Paddington branch and Grand Union Regents Canal, River Thames.

Leicestershire Ring: 154 miles
The Grand Union Main Line, Grand Union Leicester section, River Trent, Trent & Mersey Canal, Coventry Canal, Oxford Canal.

North Pennine Ring: 184 miles
Rochdale Canal, Calder & Hebble Navigation, Aire & Calder Navigation – Wakefield section, part of the Aire & Calder Main Line, Leeds & Liverpool Canal, Bridgewater Canal.

South Pennine Ring: 69 miles
Huddersfield Narrow Canal, Rochdale Canal, Ashton Canal, Huddersfield Broad Canal, Calder & Hebble Navigation.

Stourport Ring: 85 miles
Worcester & Birmingham Canal, River Severn, Staffordshire & Worcestershire Canal, BCN Main Line.

Warwickshire Ring: 104 miles
Grand Union Main Line, Birmingham & Fazeley Canal, Coventry Canal, Oxford Canal.

You can, of course, have fun selecting your own circular cruising route.

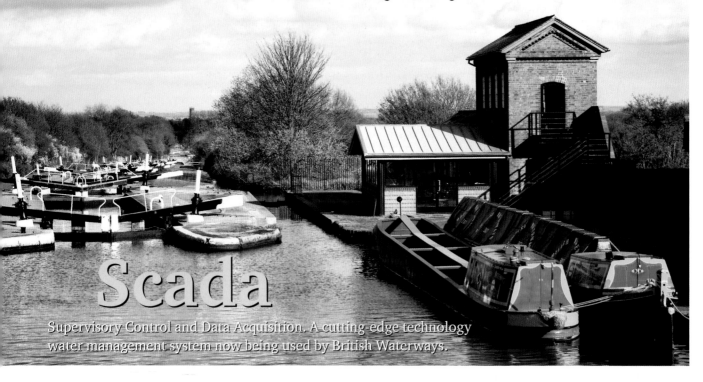

Control and planning 21st century-style!

Scada

Supervisory Control and Data Acquisition. A cutting-edge technology water management system now being used by British Waterways.

What on earth would Messrs Brindley, Smeaton, Jessup, Telford and Rennie think of a remote monitoring system able to tell them such details as how many people per hour walked past a sensor next to the towpath in Little Venice, London? British Waterways' Scada system is now well and truly up and running.

For those who don't like mysteries, the dateline at Little Venice was Tuesday 25 April 2006 and the number recorded by the Scada sensor was running at 450 when remotely polled at 14.21pm. The highest frequency of people was not surprisingly logged during what is termed the morning rush hour. And so the data rolled on. How useful are those figures and, furthermore, isn't just an ability to manage the system's water resources sufficient for BW's needs?

Not a bit of it. Ask any marketing person. Such knowledge really is power in the right hands. British Waterways have declared their intention to 'grow the business' and therefore increase revenue streams from other than the core activities of boating and angling. How could those people passing through Little Venice add to the company's income? You can bet that some marketing guru is right now pondering that very question.

Of course the big questions, which are of the greatest interest to the boating fraternity, are those concerned with water resources. Scada is able to provide 'real time answers' to questions concerning the daily tasks associated with the management of the waterways system, which is complex by nature. What it is not is a magic wand. But it comes very close to being one.

What it does is identify problems and, in some cases, offer solutions based on tried and tested models themselves based on data from many years of canal and river system management. In a worst-case scenario, when perhaps the water is just not available, no computer system can be expected to fix things. But what Scada can and does do is flag up very early warning signs and allow the section managers to look for alternative ways of keeping the boat traffic moving.

There are currently more than 550 locations connected to the Scada system and more are being added as the system is rolled out eventually to cover the whole of the waterway network controlled by British Waterways. If it is considered desirable, contractors working on the behalf of BW can be provided with a less interactive version of the data display system.

Apart from computer terminals in the 10 regional business centre offices showing the all-important live data concerning water levels, boat movements etc, the BW people on the ground can also access the information at any time. If you happen to see a waterways employee looking interested at his mobile phone, please don't report him for playing electronic games in working time!

Each of the handsets is configured so as to allow 'real time' access to Scada information. When connected, their Wap-enabled Nokia 6230s can, via a secure dedicated server, receive detailed information and display it on a miniature version of the Scada system's screen. They can dial up to see, for example, how a weir is operating at a remote location on their particular patch. In some instances, they can make a water control change electronically.

If there is, say, a particularly high instance of 'locking' on a given stretch, they are able to see exactly what effect that water usage is having on the levels in the associated pounds and ultimately on the supply network.

When any action is being taken 'on the plot', the main Scada control centre can see what is going on and the experts working there are accordingly able to offer advice and practical help if called on to do so.

No longer does water management just depend on a local supervisor or lock keeper being in the right place at the right time. The wet-finger-in-the-wind days appear to have been confined to history following the introduction and use by BW of this data-gathering system.

Furthermore, Scada has already enabled British Waterways to make appreciable energy savings by identifying and highlighting optimum pumping times and allowing the use of off-peak electricity. By its very nature the system has also meant that manpower utilisation can be more flexible and therefore more easily directed to the right place, and at the right time. It is considered by BW to be money well spent at a reported cost of £8.5-million.

As for contingency planning, if British Waterways have been made aware of a future event, they are able, by polling the Scada system, to check water supplies in the reservoirs etc, and therefore can endeavour to get enough water into a particular canal in order to maintain the efficient 'locking' of craft etc.

British Waterways has an extensive water supply network which interfaces with the major river basins of the UK, like the Severn and Trent. The company has at its disposal every day more than 2000 megalitres of water, which would rank it in the top five of UK water companies. BW now own 92 reservoirs making them the fourth-largest reservoir owner in the UK. Other water supplies under BW control include direct river abstractions, controlled feeders, uncontrolled feeders, ground water and effluent discharge.

One of their latest directives concerns the implementation of a policy devised within their commercial department, which calls for the creation of some 11,700 new berths over the next 10 years. That policy, if it is to succeed, will mean the development of a large number of new marinas.

If there is not enough water available in a particular location, then clearly it would be pointless building a marina there. BW are able to see from their current (and past) statistics exactly the number of boat movements and their effect on the water stock, and can accurately advise the planning decision-makers of their findings. In fact they would be able to use Scada-gathered data to create a model in order to ascertain if, for example, in a particular instance 'back pumping' would be the acceptable solution.

By looking at such predictive sequences, British Waterways engineers have been able to make some interesting and accurate predictions which, in themselves, can be very important when developing future water management strategy. Such predictions become even more powerful management tools when they are combined with other planning data.

As for what those great canal builders of the past would have thought of Scada, they probably would have been impressed but pointed out that they built the system, and all of its engineering wonders, without the use of a single mechanical shovel! W

Above left: In order to keep scenes like this possible, water management and control is essential. A typical summer scene on the Shroppie Middlewich branch at Wardle Lock. Author.

The Broads

Hickling Broad is the largest of all the Norfolk Broads, and it has a spectacular variety of plants and animals. It is a fascinating place, especially for those interested in swallowtail butterflies, bitterns and marsh harriers. The two-hour Water Trail runs from mid-May to mid-September, takes you into the quiet backwaters of the Broad and gives access to the Tree Tower, from which you get the most fabulous views of Broadland. Call 01692 598276 to book a place. Broads Authority.

Attracting millions of visitors every year, the Norfolk and Suffolk Broads would figure highly on anyone's list of European waterway treasures. The Broads lie to the east of Norwich and there are more than 30 of them that are, in the main, interconnected by some 200 miles of navigable rivers.

This comprehensive waterways touring system is not connected to any of Britain's other inland waterway systems, however, but all of it can be cruised without having to negotiate one single lock. On this large inland waterway there are none, except of course where the Broads meet the North Sea. The entire Broads are tidal waters, so knowledge of the tides is essential if the visiting boater is to be able to negotiate the lower bridges crossing the system.

In particular, there is a famously difficult-to-negotiate old road bridge at Potter Heigham, on the River Thurle leading to Hickling Broad. The semi-circular central arch is only 6ft 9in high in its centre and slopes sharply to either side. Hire craft wishing to negotiate the bridge are required to make use of the free services of a pilot. In high summer, boats negotiating the span provide a big free visitor attraction, with crowds gathering in order to marvel at the skills of the pilots.

The waterway is made up of seven interconnected rivers, the three principal ones being the Yare, Bure and Waveney and the smaller the Ant, Chet, Thurne and Wensum. The main rivers converge and discharge into

Breydon Water near Great Yarmouth and thereafter the whole system discharges into the North Sea.

You could, of course, be excused for thinking that this vast and beautiful expanse of wetlands was entirely created by nature – however, it was not! Only in the 1960s was evidence uncovered thath proved beyond doubt that the Broads were, to a great extent, man-made.

The area was actually the location for vast mediaeval peat- digging activities, when that naturally occurring organic material was a vital source of fuel in England. The ingress of sea water then flooded the ancient diggings. The Romans were also visitors to the area we now call the Broads and they are known to have set up harbours there in order to trade with Rome.

From the early 14th century people began to build embankments along the Broadland rivers in order to prevent them from flooding the surrounding land. A large number of wind pumps (often confused with windmills) were built to help drain the land by lifting water from the surrounding marshes and discharging it into the flowing rivers. In the modern day that activity still continues, but now using powerful diesel engines and electric motors. It is not unusual to come across small huts throughout the area that have been built especially to house the all-important drainage equipment.

In the 18th and 19th centuries the rivers of the region were altered to suit the needs of local boatmen and, as well as dredging and widening, course alterations were also carried

Above left: Canadian canoeing on the Broads. Broads Authority.

Above right: There are now said to be in the region of 100 boats for hire for every kilometre of navigable water. Author.

Above: A thatcher at work beside Wroxham Broad. Norfolk reed is reputedly the finest in the world. Author.

out. A good example of that work is the straight channel cut between Ant mouth and Fleet Dyke, which was done to avoid a huge meander in the natural course of the River Bure.

Like all the waterways of these islands, the Broads' importance as commercial trade routes declined with the coming of the railways and improvements in road transport during the earlier part of the 20th century.

However, the region did see the development of a special form of river boat. The shallow-draught Norfolk wherry was once an important trading vessel, clinker built with a strong hull and constructed mostly of oak.

Even before the decline of trade, the Broads region was recognised as a 'water play park' by both the Victorians and the Edwardians, who visited in large numbers. Regattas, otherwise known as 'water frolics', were said to have been commonplace.

Holidaying afloat was destined to be a big business on the Broads and John Loynes started his firm at Wroxham Bridge in 1879. In 1908 he was persuaded by a gentleman called Harry Blake to advertise his craft for hire to the people of London. Blake as a consequence became the firm's agent and produced their first brochure in 1908. By 1939 that hire fleet totalled 310 cruisers and 277 yachts.

In 1949 that pioneering company was joined by another destined to become a household name in the UK, Hoseasons. Between the two firms they had, by the early 1980s, increased the number of craft for hire on the Broads to a staggering 2150 cabin cruisers, 109 yachts and 450 day-hire boats.

There are now said to be 100 boats for hire for every kilometre of navigable water, as well as at least 5600 privately owned boats based on the Broads. Wroxam was the first town to develop as a hire centre and to this day it is still thought of as being the 'capital of the Broads'.

The Broads are famous for their proliferation of reed beds and sedges but those plants are not just left naturally to occur. If the beds were left unattended they would be overrun by other, more prolific species and so, because of their value as thatch, they are carefully managed. Norfolk reed is reputably the finest in the world.

From the cream-bordered green pea moth to the swan, the Broads are home to many beautiful wild creatures. If you have a keen eye and are lucky enough, birds like the bittern and

Left: A typical Broads cruiser. Author.

Below: A sail boat on Wroxham Broad. Author.

sedge warbler can be seen. And perhaps you might be fortunate enough to hear the distinctive squeal-like call of the water rail.

The area is a veritable anglers' paradise and, getting away from the busy main channels, it is possible to find coarse fishing to rival the very best in the UK. The main species include bream, perch, roach, rudd and, of course, the ubiquitous pike. Visitors are also reminded to look out for butterflies and, in particular, the swallowtail – with a wingspan of over 7cm, it is the largest in Britain.

The Broads was designated a National Park in only 1959 and was then placed under the control of the Broads Authority. The members who sit on the Broads Authority are appointed from local councils and by the Secretary of State for the Environment. The authority was set up by the Broads Act. **W**

The main Broads

Barton
Braydon Water
Filby
Hickling
Lily
Martham
Ormesby
Oulton
Rockland
Rollesby
Salthouse
Surlingham
Wroxham

■ Find out more about the body at
www.broads-authority.gov.uk

Stay safe on the water

All photographs by Ralph Freeman.

These pages have been compiled to commemorate the life of a well-known and much-loved canal personality, the late Kevin Scragg. He was known by all on the canals of the north-west and the Midlands of England (and even beyond) simply as 'Scraggy'. Together with his wife, Viv, he had, during his regrettably all-too-short life, travelled over all of the canals he loved.

Scraggy contributed to the well-being of the waterway system on almost every day of his life for, not only were he and Viv live-aboard boaters, he was also a very hard-working and well-respected canal contractor. In addition to his great love of the canals, Kev was also an avid biker, and his love affair with Harley-Davidsons was well known.

In addition to his boat restoration work he was also an accomplished artist and had planned to convert the butty Grimsby into a touring art studio.

The pair had bought the historic ex-FMC narrow boat Monarch and had then set about tailoring it to meet their personal requirements. It had been fitted with a new diesel engine and Scraggy's next project was to complete the restoration of the butty and then take the matched pair to wherever the fancy took him and Viv.

We may never know exactly what brought Kev's life to such an abrupt end but what we do know is that it was probably a lethal toxin that accidentally entered his body while he was carrying out dredging work. The initial thoughts were that Scraggy had possibly succumbed to Weil's disease, a waterborne killer of which all who work or travel on the slower-moving waterways need to be aware.

Simply in memory of Kevin Scragg, take the time to read the warnings about leptospirosis, Weil's disease and other waterborne dangers in the relevant British Waterways and Waterways Ireland publications. Scraggy made his last journey by narrow boat at Fradley Junction on 12 October 2005. He was 42 years old. He will be sorely missed by a great many. **W**

■ There is a worldwide Leptospirosis Information Centre that you can contact to read more. It can be found at www.leptospirosis.org

Visit Salford

Reader Offer

Home to the world's first steam boat, over 30 miles of rivers & canals, Oh! and a certain Mr Lowry.

There's more to Salford than its favourite son and those matchstick cats n dogs.

Try idyllic Worsley village, home to 53 miles of underground canals, the world's first steam boat and the transport revolution for starters!

Get a set of three new Salford self-guided walks for the exclusive price of £5, a massive 33% off. Just call 0161 848 8601 and quote: Waterways

Your journey starts here: www.visitsalford.info/industrialheritage

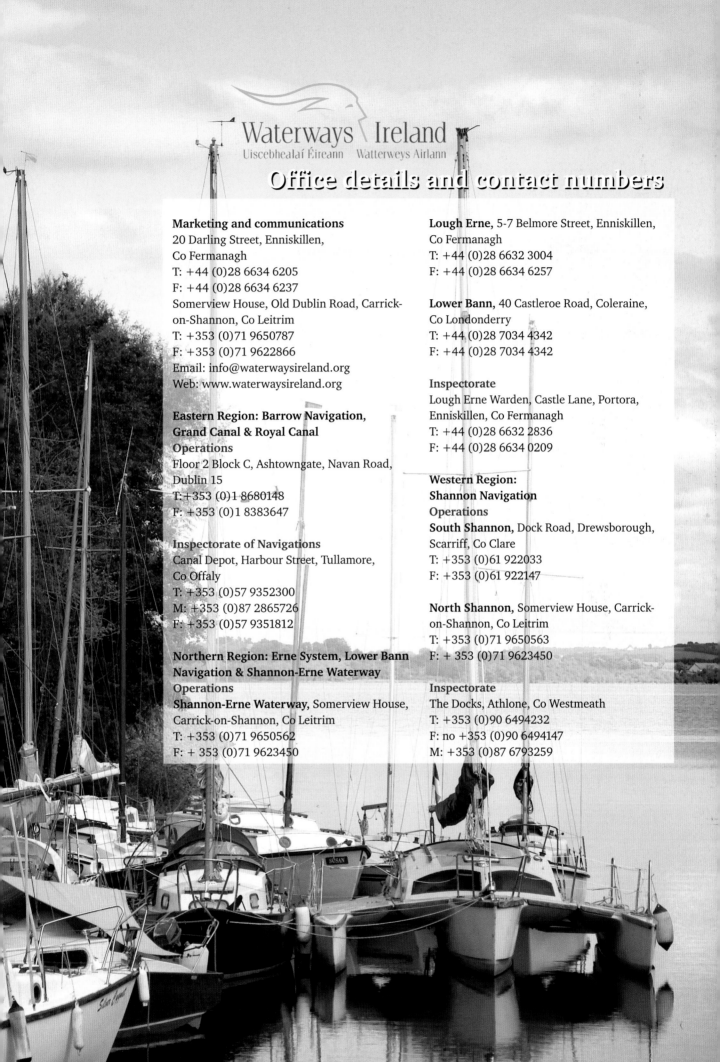

![Waterways Ireland / Uiscebhealaí Éireann / Watterweys Airlann]

Office details and contact numbers

Marketing and communications
20 Darling Street, Enniskillen,
Co Fermanagh
T: +44 (0)28 6634 6205
F: +44 (0)28 6634 6237
Somerview House, Old Dublin Road, Carrick-on-Shannon, Co Leitrim
T: +353 (0)71 9650787
F: +353 (0)71 9622866
Email: info@waterwaysireland.org
Web: www.waterwaysireland.org

Eastern Region: Barrow Navigation, Grand Canal & Royal Canal
Operations
Floor 2 Block C, Ashtowngate, Navan Road, Dublin 15
T: +353 (0)1 8680148
F: +353 (0)1 8383647

Inspectorate of Navigations
Canal Depot, Harbour Street, Tullamore, Co Offaly
T: +353 (0)57 9352300
M: +353 (0)87 2865726
F: +353 (0)57 9351812

Northern Region: Erne System, Lower Bann Navigation & Shannon-Erne Waterway
Operations
Shannon-Erne Waterway, Somerview House, Carrick-on-Shannon, Co Leitrim
T: +353 (0)71 9650562
F: + 353 (0)71 9623450

Lough Erne, 5-7 Belmore Street, Enniskillen, Co Fermanagh
T: +44 (0)28 6632 3004
F: +44 (0)28 6634 6257

Lower Bann, 40 Castleroe Road, Coleraine, Co Londonderry
T: +44 (0)28 7034 4342
F: +44 (0)28 7034 4342

Inspectorate
Lough Erne Warden, Castle Lane, Portora, Enniskillen, Co Fermanagh
T: +44 (0)28 6632 2836
F: +44 (0)28 6634 0209

Western Region:
Shannon Navigation
Operations
South Shannon, Dock Road, Drewsborough, Scarriff, Co Clare
T: +353 (0)61 922033
F: +353 (0)61 922147

North Shannon, Somerview House, Carrick-on-Shannon, Co Leitrim
T: +353 (0)71 9650563
F: + 353 (0)71 9623450

Inspectorate
The Docks, Athlone, Co Westmeath
T: +353 (0)90 6494232
F: no +353 (0)90 6494147
M: +353 (0)87 6793259

British Waterways
Office details and contact numbers

Customer Service Centre
Willow Grange, Church Road,
Watford WD17 4QA
T: 01923 201120
F: 01923 201304
enquiries.hq@britishwaterways.co.uk

For information on visiting the waterways,
including great days out, go to:
www.waterscape.com or for corporate
information go to
www.britishwaterways.co.uk

Head office
Willow Grange, Church Road,
Watford WD17 4QA
T: 01923 226422

South East Waterways
Ground Floor, 500-600 Witan Gate, Central
Milton Keynes MK9 1BW
T: 01908 302500
F: 01908 302510
enquiries.southeast@britishwaterways.co.uk

South West Waterways
Harbour House, West Quay, The Docks,
Gloucester GL21 2LG
T: 01452 318000
F: 01 452 318076
enquiries.southwest@britishwaterways.co.uk

West Midlands Waterways
Albert House, Quay Place, 92-93 Edward
Street, Birmingham B1 2RA
T: 0121 200 7400
F: 0121 200 7401
enquiries.westmidlands@
britishwaterways.co.uk

Central Shires Waterways
Peel's Wharf, Lichfield Street, Fazeley,
Tamworth B78 3QZ
T: 01827 252000
F: 01827 288071
enquiries.centralshires
@britishwaterways.co.uk

East Midlands Waterways
The Kiln, Mather Road, Newark,
Nottinghamshire NG24 1FB
T: 01636 704481
F: 01636 705584
enquiries.eastmidlands
@britishwaterways.co.uk

Yorkshire Waterways
Fearns Wharf, Neptune Street, Leeds LS9 8PB
T: 0113 2816800
F: 0113 281 6886
enquiries.yorkshire@britishwaterways.co.uk

Wales & Border Counties Waterways
Navigation Road, Northwich,
Cheshire CW8 1BH
T: 01606 723800
F: 01606 871471
enquiries.wbc@britishwaterways.co.uk

North West Waterways
Waterside House, Waterside Drive,
Wigan WN3 5AZ
T: 01942 405700
F: 01942 405710
enquiries.northwest@britishwaterways.co.uk

British Waterways London
1 Sheldon Square, Paddington Central,
London W2 6TT
T: 020 7985 7200
F: 020 7985 7201
enquiries.london@britishwaterways.co.uk

British Waterways Scotland
Canal House, Applecross Street,
Glasgow G4 9SP
T: 0141 332 6936
F: 0141 331 1688
enquiries.scotland@britishwaterways.co.uk